ICNC **MONOGRAPH** SERIES

# Civil Resistance Against Climate Change

Robyn Gulliver, Kelly S. Fielding, Winnifred R. Louis

# Contents

**Executive Summary** .................................................................. 1

**Introduction** ........................................................................ 3

    Research Questions and Objectives ........................................ 5

    What is Civil Resistance? ..................................................... 6

    Data and Methodology ......................................................... 9

    Monograph Structure .......................................................... 11

**Chapter 1: The Emergence of Civil Resistance Against Climate Change** ......... 12

    Climate Change as a Global Issue ........................................... 12

    The Emergence of Civil Resistance Against Climate Change ............. 12

    Movement Frameworks ....................................................... 14

        Great Turning Model ................................................... 15

        Climate Insurgency Model ............................................ 17

        The Political Process Model .......................................... 18

    Summary ......................................................................... 21

**Chapter 2: The Australian Climate Change Civil Resistance Movement** .......... 22

    The Australian Context ....................................................... 23

    Data Collection, Methodology, and Analysis ............................... 24

    Climate Change Activism Within the Australian Environmental Movement .... 26

        The Emergence of Environmental and Climate Change Groups ..... 26

        Organizational Structures ............................................ 27

        Framing of Environmental and Climate Issues ..................... 29

        Events and Civil Resistance Tactics ................................. 31

        Civil Resistance Tactics ............................................... 34

        Acts of Omission ...................................................... 35

        Acts of Commission ................................................... 36

    Social Creative Interventions . . . . . . . . . . . . . . . . . . . . . . . . . . . . . . . . . . . . . **36**

    Acts of Expression . . . . . . . . . . . . . . . . . . . . . . . . . . . . . . . . . . . . . . . . . . . . . . **37**

    Organizational Status and Civil Resistance Tactics . . . . . . . . . . . . . . . . . . . . . . **37**

    Outcomes of Climate Change Campaigns . . . . . . . . . . . . . . . . . . . . . . . . . . . . **39**

  Key Insights and Discussion . . . . . . . . . . . . . . . . . . . . . . . . . . . . . . . . . . . . . . . . . . **42**

## Chapter 3: Case Studies of Anti-Corporate Civil Resistance Campaigns . . . . . . . . . . . **45**

  Case Study 1: The Stop Adani Campaign . . . . . . . . . . . . . . . . . . . . . . . . . . . . . . . . . **47**

    Case Study Data and Analysis . . . . . . . . . . . . . . . . . . . . . . . . . . . . . . . . . . . . . . **49**

    Groups Active in the Stop Adani Campaign . . . . . . . . . . . . . . . . . . . . . . . . . . . **50**

    Tactics Used by Groups Active in the Stop Adani Campaign . . . . . . . . . . . . . . **51**

    Primary and Secondary Targets . . . . . . . . . . . . . . . . . . . . . . . . . . . . . . . . . . . . **54**

    Outcomes of Civil Resistance Tactics Against Secondary Targets . . . . . . . . . . . **56**

  Case Study 2: The Divestment Campaign . . . . . . . . . . . . . . . . . . . . . . . . . . . . . . . . **58**

    Case Study Data and Analysis . . . . . . . . . . . . . . . . . . . . . . . . . . . . . . . . . . . . . . **60**

    Groups Active in the Divestment Campaign . . . . . . . . . . . . . . . . . . . . . . . . . . . **60**

    Tactics Used in the Divestment Campaign . . . . . . . . . . . . . . . . . . . . . . . . . . . . **62**

    Targets and Outcomes . . . . . . . . . . . . . . . . . . . . . . . . . . . . . . . . . . . . . . . . . . . **63**

  Case Study Insights and Discussion . . . . . . . . . . . . . . . . . . . . . . . . . . . . . . . . . . . . **66**

## Chapter 4: State Responses to Disruptive Civil Resistance . . . . . . . . . . . . . . . . . . . . . **71**

  Investigating State Repression . . . . . . . . . . . . . . . . . . . . . . . . . . . . . . . . . . . . . . . . **72**

    Disruptive Civil Resistance Tactics and Government Responses . . . . . . . . . . . **73**

  Insights and Key Findings on State Responses . . . . . . . . . . . . . . . . . . . . . . . . . . . . **76**

## Chapter 5: Mapping Climate Change Civil Resistance
## onto Movement Frameworks . . . . . . . . . . . . . . . . . . . . . . . . . . . . . . . . . . . . . . . . . . . **78**

  Macy's Great Turning . . . . . . . . . . . . . . . . . . . . . . . . . . . . . . . . . . . . . . . . . . . . . . . . **78**

    Component 1: Holding Actions, Resisting . . . . . . . . . . . . . . . . . . . . . . . . . . . . . **78**

    Component 2: Creating Alternative Structures . . . . . . . . . . . . . . . . . . . . . . . . . **79**

      Component 3: Shift in Consciousness and Values .................... 79

      Summary of the Great Turning Model .......................... 79

   Brecher's Climate Insurgency ..................................... 80

      Component 1: An Insurgency of Civil Resistance .................. 80

      Component 2: Legal Arguments and Litigation ................... 81

      Component 3: Self-Organization and Deisolation ................. 81

      Summary of the Climate Insurgency Model ..................... 82

   Political Process Model .......................................... 82

      Component 1: Political Opportunities ........................... 83

      Component 2: Mobilizing Structures ........................... 83

      Component 3: Framing ...................................... 84

      Summary for Political Process Model .......................... 85

   Insights from the Application of These Models ....................... 85

## Chapter 6: Takeaways for Specific Groups .............................. 86

   Activists and Civil Society Groups .................................. 86

   Academics and Researchers ...................................... 88

   External Actors: The Public and the International Community ........... 89

   Final Remarks .................................................. 91

## References ......................................................... 92

## Methodological Appendix ............................................ 102

   Groups Database: Identification of Australian Groups Focusing
on Environmental Advocacy ...................................... 102

   Campaigns and Outcomes Databases: Identification
of Climate Change-Related Campaigns and Their Outcomes ........... 104

   Tactics Database: Categorization of All Tactics Used
by Environmental Groups in the Study Population ................... 104

   Civil Resistance Tactics Database: Identification
and Categorization of Civil Resistance Tactics ....................... 106

## Tables and Figures

TABLE 1. Categories and Examples of Civil Resistance .................... 8

TABLE 2. Terms, Definitions, and Data Used in This Monograph .................... 10

TABLE 3. Event Categories, Descriptions, and Examples .................... 25

TABLE 4. Organizational Status of Environmental Groups and Sub-Groups .................... 28

TABLE 5. Frequency of Words Related to Climate, Justice, Conservation, and Sustainability Occurring on Environmental Group Websites .................... 29

TABLE 6. Climate Change Topics and Most Frequent Words in Environmental Group Websites .................... 30

TABLE 7. Unique Civil Resistance Tactics, Ordered by Category, 2010–2019 .................... 35

TABLE 8. Number of Civil Resistance Tactics Promoted by Umbrella Groups .................... 38

TABLE 9. Outcomes of Climate Change Campaigns, 2017–2020 .................... 42

TABLE 10. Examples of Campaign Goals, Targets, and Outcomes .................... 42

TABLE 11. Groups Involved in the Stop Adani Campaign .................... 50

TABLE 12. Events Promoted by Groups Active in the Stop Adani Campaign .................... 51

TABLE 13. Stop Adani Events Aligned with Categories of Civil Resistance .................... 53

TABLE 14. Most Common Targets Identified in Facebook Event Text .................... 55

TABLE 15. Number of Secondary Targets by Sector .................... 57

TABLE 16. Selection of Wins Against Government Secondary Targets .................... 58

TABLE 17. The Divestment Campaign: Groups, Sub-Groups, Their Status, Civil Resistance Tactics Used, and Number of Events Associated with Each .................... 61

TABLE 18. Range of Events Promoted in Divestment Campaign (Including Cohosted Events) .................... 62

TABLE 19. Types of Civil Resistance Used in the Divestment Campaign .................... 63

TABLE 20. Australian Divestment Targets and Announcements by Organization Type, 2015–2019 .................... 64

TABLE 21. Government Responses to Disruptive Civil Resistance .................... 74

| | |
|---|---|
| TABLE 22. Mapping Data onto the Components of the Great Turning | 78 |
| TABLE 23. Mapping Data onto the Components of the Climate Insurgency | 80 |
| TABLE 24. Mapping Data onto the Components of the Political Process Model | 82 |
| FIGURE 1. Three Components of the Great Turning | 15 |
| FIGURE 2. Great Turning Components and Data to Be Mapped onto Each Component | 16 |
| FIGURE 3. Climate Insurgency Components and Data to Be Mapped onto Each Component | 18 |
| FIGURE 4. Political Process Model Components and Data to Be Mapped onto Each Component | 20 |
| FIGURE 5. Information Presented in This Chapter | 22 |
| FIGURE 6. Emergence of Environmental Activism Groups in Australia | 27 |
| FIGURE 7. Words Most Commonly Associated with Climate Topics in Environmental Group Websites | 31 |
| FIGURE 8. Comparison of Conventional and Directed Network Campaign Structures | 32 |
| FIGURE 9. All Unique Events by Group Category, 2010–2019 | 32 |
| FIGURE 10. Types of Event Promoted by Environmental Groups | 33 |
| FIGURE 11. Most Common Civil Resistance Tactics, All Environmental Groups, 2010–2019 | 34 |
| FIGURE 12. Climate Angels at Extinction Rebellion Declaration Day | 39 |
| FIGURE 13. Location of the Galilee Basin, Queensland | 47 |
| FIGURE 14. Stop Adani Logos at the School Strike for Climate Event | 52 |
| FIGURE 15. Human Sign Action | 54 |
| FIGURE 16. Change in Stop Adani Targets over Time | 56 |

FIGURE 17. **Divestment Campaign Events and Divestment Announcements, 2014–2019** . . . . . . . . . . . . . . . . . . . . . . . . . . . . . . . . . . **65**

FIGURE 18. **Climate Activism Arrests, Broken Down Across States, 2016–2019** . . . . . . . . . . . . . . . . . . . . . . . . . . . . . . . . . . **73**

# Executive Summary

Our rapidly changing climate poses one of the greatest threats to humanity. As we veer closer to climate tipping points with the potential for irreversible damage to major ecosystems, people around the world are demanding urgent action. The recent rise of groups focused on climate change such as Extinction Rebellion and School Strike for Climate have been presaged by over two decades of transnational climate activism engaging a diverse range of actors across the global north and south, and involving a vibrant mix of strategies and tactics. But to what extent do these activists incorporate civil resistance—that is, nonviolent, extra-institutional, conflict-waging tactics—into their tactical repertoire? Further, to the extent that civil resistance against climate change is happening, what does it look like, and to what extent is it achieving its goals?

This monograph seeks to answer these questions by presenting an empirical analysis of the Australian climate change movement. Using three movement frameworks as a theoretical foundation, it begins with an overview of the broader environmental movement before considering the types of groups engaging in civil resistance against climate change, the range of actions they undertake, and the targets they seek to influence. It then examines two campaigns directed at corporate targets—the Stop Adani anti-coal mining campaign, and the Divestment campaign—as case studies before considering the extent to which civil resistance in Australia is prompting repressive responses from the state. It offers key lessons for a range of individuals and groups, from climate activists and civil society organizations to academics and others interested in supporting nonviolent action against climate change. In doing so, it addresses major gaps in our understanding of the effectiveness of civil resistance against climate change and the potential this resistance holds to prompt urgent action.

Our analysis finds that the Australian climate change movement is capitalizing on opportunities to create change by rapidly creating a multitude of flexible, grassroots groups which collectively engage in a multiplicity of diverse tactics and campaigns. These tactics include sharing information about climate change, building localized alternative social and economic structures, and obtaining climate change action commitments from organizations, as well as sustained, targeted civil resistance. The two case studies demonstrate that waging civil resistance has achieved some success, including substantially delaying new coal mines, securing divestment commitments, and strengthening the movement at large. However, despite these successes, Australia's response to the climate crisis remains woefully inadequate. As such, we hope this monograph prompts further analysis of civil resistance against climate change to help identify the most effective strategies for urgently addressing our global climate emergency.

# Introduction

Since 1988, the Intergovernmental Panel on Climate Change (IPCC) has produced numerous reports describing the latest scientific information on the progress and risks of human-induced climate change. Each report details a range of possible responses as year after year the projections and risks become more critical. This looming crisis is built on past failures to address environmental issues, such as rising global extinction rates and biodiversity loss, water shortages, and deforestation (Rich 2018; Ripple et al., 2017). Yet the message that urgent action is needed has largely gone unheeded. With few exceptions, governments around the world have proven unable or unwilling to enact the policies required to reverse the escalating emissions causing human-induced climate change. Although some policies may have slowed the accelerating pace of climate change, policies that have been introduced to date have failed to stabilize the climate, with the latest IPCC report itemizing consistent environmental declines (IPCC 2018).

In response to this lack of progress, countless citizens have demanded urgent and meaningful action to address climate change. Activism, fueled by outrage and urgency, is advancing the global movement at a dramatic speed. Since 2015, increasingly radical forms of resistance have emerged to challenge the status quo, using a diverse range of tactics directed at a range of targets, including corporations, investment funds, and government bodies. This activity follows years of intensifying activism against climate change, from the late 1990s onward. Since that time, individuals and their networks have contested the development of fossil fuel projects and pipelines, promoted local, grassroots initiatives for climate action and resilience, and coordinated international days of climate action that incorporate events ranging from blockades to bike rides and mass rallies.

Climate change groups and networks have emerged in different contexts across the globe, resulting in a rich diversity of climate activism. In Australia and New Zealand, concern about climate change consequences has coalesced around the impact of large development projects (O'Brien 2013). Climate activism in other developed nations such as the UK and Germany has emerged out of antiwar and anti-nuclear movements (Graham-Leigh 2014; Koessler 2014). While some argue that environmental groups and activists in the United States have historically neglected issues of race and justice, climate activism in that country has deep roots in the environmental justice and civil rights movements (Dawson 2010). Calls for climate justice emerged out of the environmental justice framework that identified unjust impacts of climate change as another example of inequality and social injustice (Schlosberg and Collins 2014). In the global south, climate change has intersected with anti-globalization and anti-poverty issues (Chatterton et al. 2013). Thus, there is a huge diversity of actors and actions that together comprise the civil sector response to climate change.

In this monograph, we refer to this collective of actors and actions as the "climate movement." In doing so we follow Giugni and Grasso (2015), who define a movement through three characteristics: first, that individuals share a collective identity; second, that they interact in a loose network of organizations with varying degrees of formality; and third, that they are engaged voluntarily in collective action motivated by shared concern about an issue. Movements engage in different forms of contestation (Cox and Pezzullo 2016), one of which is a campaign, that is, a "thematically, socially, and temporally interconnected series of interactions that ... are geared to a specific goal" (Porta and Rucht 2002, 3). Campaigns can have a range of goals and use diverse tactical repertoires. What unites collective actors together as a movement—whether as groups or individuals (Tarrow 2011)—is their shared identity as advocates (Diani 1992).

*As the climate movement emerges and grows, there has been evidence of restrictive and defensive government responses, including bans on climate protest and new police powers intended to suppress protest.*

Our aim in the monograph is to consider the tactics used by the Australian climate movement broadly, as well as to specifically focus on the characteristics of civil resistance actions. We then draw on social change frameworks to investigate the climate movement's potential to achieve its goals. We focus on two frameworks that have been specifically applied to environmental change: Joanna Macy's three stages of the Great Turning (Macy 2007) and Jeremy Brecher's climate insurgency model (2015). We also focus on the political process model (McAdam 1982; Tilly 1978) due to its prevalence within the academic literature on social change. We consider these frameworks and the extent to which our data maps onto them to identify areas of strength and weakness in the climate change movement.

This monograph also investigates how those responsible for emissions—namely, governments and corporations—are responding to civil resistance against climate change. Around the world a preference for attributing blame for climate change to consumer choices enables some governments and corporations to deflect the focus from systems-level policy change so that they can continue extractive "business as usual" polluting practices with the argument that humanity can buy its way out of environmental collapse (Wicker 2017). However, there is a growing response that individual behavior change is insufficient to address environmental problems (see Jackson 2009; Seyfang 2009; Abrash Walton 2018b). Some newer groups such as Extinction Rebellion now explicitly call for systems change over mere behavior change, using innovative mass civil resistance to convey their message. These activities, alongside the dire threat that a zero emissions goal presents to some of the largest corporations in the world, appear to have resulted in similar responses from industries and corporations as those used by the tobacco industry to respond to the association of their product with lung cancer. That is, the corporations have responded with attempts to delay government action through financing think tanks to disseminate junk science, sowing doubt about links between tobacco and cancer (or in this case, human activity and climate change), and blocking government regulations (see Oreskes and Conway 2011). Furthermore, even where corporations are being held responsible and government action is occurring, the changes have not successfully targeted the largest emitters. For example, while 60 countries have announced a net zero emission goal by 2050, these countries only account for 11 percent of global emissions (Sengupta and Popovich 2019). In addition, as the climate movement emerges and grows, there has been evidence of restrictive and defensive government responses in countries such as Australia, the United States, and the United Kingdom, including bans on climate protest (Meredith 2019) and new police powers intended to suppress protest (Schomberg and Dawson 2019).

## Research Questions and Objectives

The objective of this monograph is to advance knowledge about civil resistance against climate change, using the Australian climate movement as a case study. Australia offers a rich context to undertake this work. As an advanced democracy, activism in Australia is both communicated and undertaken in relative freedom, while citizens enjoy widespread access to digital communications. Furthermore, Australia is on the forefront of experiencing climate impacts. These qualities present a unique opportunity to gather extensive empirical data on the characteristics and outcomes of civil resistance against climate change at a national level.

In the past, comparatively little empirical data capturing the full range and features of the climate movement's use of civil resistance has been available to either activists or academics. As such, the characteristics and outcomes of civil resistance tactics used by climate change groups are largely unknown. To help fill this gap, this study uses a large dataset about the Australian environmental movement to investigate what civil resistance against climate change looks like, who it targets, what it achieves, and how it is evolving and adapting to external and internal pressures.

The dataset is first presented to provide an overview of the issues and activities that environmental groups in general are engaged in. We then delve into the tactics promoted by these groups and, separately and more specifically, into civil resistance tactics used by groups focusing on climate change. We classify the civil resistance tactics following Beer's (2021) categorization of nonviolent action and investigate the extent to which climate change campaigns and civil resistance tactics are successful at achieving campaign goals. We then consider the extent to which these tactics may lead to successful campaign outcomes via two specific case studies: the Stop Adani[1] and Divestment campaigns. We then map our data onto movement frameworks, allowing us to identify the extent to which the Australian climate change civil resistance movement may be advancing the global climate movement's goals. In this monograph we provide an empirical foundation to evaluate the effectiveness of climate change civil resistance tactics and offer suggestions for driving more urgent and meaningful action on climate change. Through this process we address the following questions:

- What does civil resistance against climate change in the Australian environmental movement look like? How is it connected to the wider Australian environmental movement network?

- Do civil resistance tactics and outcomes map onto key social and environmental movement theoretical frameworks?

- What groups in Australia engage in civil resistance against climate change and how are they and their allies targeting multinational corporations and associated entities? Which tactics have been most effective in driving change against corporate targets?

- Are governments pushing back against civil resistance and has this changed over time?

## What is Civil Resistance?

In this monograph we situate civil resistance under the umbrella term "activism." Entities engaging in activism can include any grassroots or civil society social mobilization organizations which seek to change or protect laws, policies, practices, powerholders, and structures of the state, corporate, and cultural spheres in any given society. Activism can take many forms, with a large body of research grouping actions into two broad categories: conventional (or institutional) actions, and radical (or extra-institutional) actions (see Moskalenko and McCauley 2009; Tausch et al. 2011; Wright, Taylor, and Moghaddam 1990). The first category encompasses actions using conventional or institutional channels to create social or political change; these include tactics such as lobbying, legal challenges, and educational events aiming to raise public awareness of a particular issue. The second category comprises extra-institutional means such as violent actions and civil resistance, the latter of which uses nonviolent actions outside of conventional channels (Bartkowski and Merriman 2016).

---

1     The Adani coal mine is a large, proposed coal mine in northern Queensland which is controversial because of the extent to which it will increase carbon emissions and expand coal production (Russo 2018). Adani company changed its name to 'Bravus' in 2020, but for clarity we use the name 'Adani' throughout this Monograph. The campaign against the mine is the focus of our first case study considered in Chapter 4.

Institutional channels of change—such as voting, lobbying, and litigation (Burkett 2016)—and extra-institutional violent and civil resistance tactics can all be potential parts of any movement's tactical repertoire. We follow Véronique Dudouet's definition of civil resistance as presented in the ICNC Special Report, *Powering to Peace: Integrated Civil Resistance and Peacebuilding Strategies*. She argues that "Civil resistance is an extra-institutional conflict-waging strategy in which organized grassroots movements use various, strategically sequenced and planned out, nonviolent tactics such as strikes, boycotts, marches, demonstrations, noncooperation, self-organizing and constructive resistance to fight perceived injustice without the threat or use of violence" (Dudouet 2017, 5). These nonviolent tactics can encompass both visible and invisible tactics that can be economic, social, and political in nature (Bartkowski and Merriman 2016).

Research on civil resistance has focused on identifying and categorizing the many ways in which it manifests in movements across time and locations. Gene Sharp pioneered the categorization of nonviolent action in his three-volume book, *The Politics of Nonviolent Action* (1973), where he identified 198 nonviolent tactics and grouped these within three classes of methods: nonviolent protest and persuasion (e.g., public speeches and public assemblies), nonviolent cooperation in social, economic, or political arenas (e.g., boycotts and industrial strikes), and nonviolent intervention (e.g., hunger strikes and sit-ins). Overall, Sharp highlighted, nonviolent methods can involve "acts of commission, whereby people do what they are not supposed to do, not expected to do, or forbidden by law from doing; acts of omission, whereby people do not do what they are supposed to do, are expected to do, or are required by law to do; or a combination of acts of commission and omission" (Sharp 1973, 68). Since then, many scholars have used and advanced his work. In particular, technological advances and the global sharing of campaign techniques and tools have also broadened the type of actions that can fall into the repertoire of nonviolent resistance. Beer (2021) has updated these types in his ICNC monograph, *Civil Resistance Tactics in the 21st Century*, which we use as our categorization guide in this study (see Table 1, on the following page).

> *Activism can take many forms, with a large body of research grouping actions into two broad categories: conventional (or institutional) actions, and radical (or extra-institutional) actions.*

### Table 1. Categories and Examples of Civil Resistance (amended from Beer, 2021[2])

| CATEGORY | SUB-CATEGORY | TYPE | EXAMPLE |
|---|---|---|---|
| **Acts of Omission (not doing)** | Social | | Ghost town (large portions of the population stay home instead of going to work or school) |
| | Economic | Strikes | State-wide strikes |
| | | Boycotts | Divestment (institutional separation from corporations whose actions investors find objectionable) |
| | Political | | Legislative obstruction (e.g., delaying a quorum) |
| | Refraining | | Active abstention from a planned action |
| **Acts of Commission (doing or creating)** | Disruptive | Social | Public filibuster |
| | | Physical | Parliamentary/legislature/council disruption (often happens through shouting, singing, chanting) |
| | | Economic | Business whistleblowing |
| | | Psychological | Distributed denial of service (DDoS) |
| | Creative | Social | Alternative social institutions |
| | | Political/legal | Reverse trials |
| | | Physical | Critical mass (e.g., cycling swarm along streets) |
| | | Economic | Alternative economic institutions |
| | | Psychological | Self-imposed transparency (deliberate organizational transparency about ongoing affairs and issue) |
| **Acts of Expression (saying)** | Medium of electronic communication | Mass action | SMS/email/social media bombing |
| | | Crowdsourcing information | Sousveillance (covert surveillance by citizens, frequently of authorities) |
| | | Creating online digital content | Digital video and audio art |
| | | Recording and distributing news of nonviolent action | Livestreaming |
| | Medium of language | | Call-in/phone march |
| | Medium of person | Public assemblies | Coordinated worldwide demonstrations |
| | | Rituals and Traditions | Growing/shaving hair as protest |
| | | Movements and gestures | Human chain |
| | | Performance | Wearing/displaying a single color |
| | | Procession | Walks and treks |
| | Medium of things | Sound/music | Drumming |
| | | 2-Dimensional arts | Stickers |
| | | 3-Dimensional arts | Costumes |

---

2     The example tactics listed in Table 1 were sourced from the online tactics list available on the Nonviolence International website: **https://tactics.nonviolenceinternational.net/dataset**

Beer makes four additions to Sharp's categorization. First, he notes that acts of omission—not doing something that opponents of the action want them to do (e.g., not buying goods as part of an economic boycott)—can be located in social, economic, and political contexts. Second, he adds a category of refraining, which occurs when an action is called off to reward or persuade the target. Third, Beer highlights how acts of commission— doing something that opponents of the action do not want them to do (e.g., protests)—can be disruptive of the status quo or creative in attempting to shift toward a new future. Some acts of commission (such as actions against perceived illegitimate laws) can take both disruptive and creative forms. Illegal gatherings against COVID-19 lockdown regulations, for example, would be classified as disruptive. Conversely, in 2019, Extinction Rebellion Australia held citizen's assemblies to protest the inadequate legislation currently governing Australia's climate change response and to develop alternative plans for reaching net zero carbon emissions. These assemblies would be classified as creative acts of commission.

Beer also itemizes how expressions of protest can occur through different media, including electronic communication, language, the human body, and "things." Finally, he includes social and political forms of creative interventions which seek to develop alternative structures or communities. In this monograph, we aim to identify the extent to which activists engage in these social and political creative interventions.

## Data and Methodology

This study focuses on the Australian climate movement because this is our own national context. We trust that international readers will either immediately see the applicability of the analysis to their own nations or indeed be spurred to conduct or commission comparative research in their own national contexts. To understand the characteristics and objectives of the climate change civil resistance movement in Australia, we provide a broad overview of the environmental movement. We then focus on the groups fighting against climate change, and, more specifically, those groups using civil resistance tactics. As such, our data encompasses information on 492 environmental groups, 193 climate change campaigns, and 36,541 events.

Table 2 provides an overview of the data, as well as the terms and definitions used throughout the monograph. A detailed description of the methods used to identify, acquire, and code this data is provided in the Appendix, while data that this monograph relied on is publicly available online on the Open Science Framework at: **https://osf.io/f8pys/**.

### Table 2. Terms, Definitions, and Data Used in This Monograph

| TERM | DEFINITION | DATA SOURCES AND ACQUISITION PROCESSES | DATA ANALYSIS |
|---|---|---|---|
| Environmental Activism Group | Activism is operationalized through following the Australian legal definition of advocacy: "activities which are aimed at securing or opposing any change to a law, policy or practice in the Commonwealth, a state or territory, or another country" (Australian Government 2012, 1). | A search of online and government databases and networks was undertaken, from which a Group Database composed of 728 Australian groups focusing on environmental activism was constructed. We were able to scrape website full text from 492 of these groups; the remaining 237 had Facebook pages or public groups. | The website content from each of the 492 groups was downloaded and coded for key characteristics such as their primary issue, campaigns, and events. |
| Campaign | A campaign is "a connected series of operations designed to bring about a particular result" (Merriam-Webster 2021). | The website content from each group in the Group Database was read to identify campaign names, issues, goals, and targets for the Campaigns Database. | The climate change-related campaigns identified through the website text were coded for campaign target and goal. |
| Tactics | Tactics are "an action or strategy carefully planned to achieve a specific end" (Oxford Dictionary 2020). Each event type promoted by environmental groups in the dataset represents a single tactic. | All events promoted on the public Facebook pages operated by the groups in the Group Database were copied to create the Tactics Database. We also created two subsets of tactics used in the Stop Adani and Divestment case studies. | A subset of tactics focusing on climate change was created. This subset included all events organized by climate change groups and all events related to climate change. |
| Civil Resistance Tactics | "Acts of commission, whereby people do what they are not supposed to do, not expected to do, or forbidden by law from doing; acts of omissions, whereby people do not do what they are supposed to do, are expected to do, or are required by law to do; or a combination of acts of commission and omission" (Sharp 1973, 68). | All tactics in the Tactics Database were reviewed to identify those which fit Beer's (2021) categorization of the three types of nonviolent actions (see Table 1): Commission, Omission, and Expression. These were compiled into the Civil Resistance Tactics Database. | All civil resistance tactics in the Civil Resistance Tactics Database were grouped into categories, with results presented in the relevant monograph sections. |
| Outcome | "The clearly defined, decisive and achievable changes in social actors, i.e., individuals, groups, organizations or institutions that will contribute to the overall campaign goal(s)" (UN Women 2012, 1). | Internet searches for any outcomes associated with campaigns (including on the groups' own websites) were undertaken, with information found compiled into the Outcomes Database. | All online information found which related to a campaign outcome was read to code whether the campaign goal or sub-goal had been successfully achieved. |

## Monograph Structure

This monograph has six main sections following the introduction, which has presented definitions and examples of the key terms used in this monograph. In Chapter 1 a comparative review of the landscape of international civil resistance against climate change is presented. It examines how individuals around the world are coalescing into groups and engaging in civil resistance in their local communities. The chapter also outlines three theoretical frameworks to track the progression of social movements for social justice, democracy, and sustainability in order to inform strategic pathways forward for activists.

Chapter 2 provides a detailed analysis of tactics promoted by environmental and climate change groups in Australia. While the majority of these tactics use conventional methods, we identify the proportion and type of tactics that align with Beer's (2021) categories of civil resistance action. We then consider the important role that grassroots organizations play and whether their tactics differ from professional environmental organizations due to their freedom to operate outside legal constraints imposed by governments. Finally, we review the outcomes of 193 Australian climate change campaigns to identify the extent to which the climate movement is achieving its goals.

Chapter 3 analyzes two of the most well-known Australian climate campaigns targeting business interests currently underway in Australia: the Stop Adani coal mine campaign and the Divestment campaign. We consider the use of civil resistance tactics by activists and their groups in these campaigns, and the degree to which these campaigns are achieving success.

Chapter 4 presents an analysis of our dataset on civil resistance tactics and state responses over the period 2017–2019, mapped onto key moments of relevant federal and state legislative and political change. In Australia, activists have faced increased push back by all tiers of government in their use of civil resistance. After presenting data on peaks of civil resistance by climate activists, we identify the mechanisms used by government to restrict this activism.

Chapter 5 maps the key findings from the data presented in Chapters 1–4 onto the three movement frameworks. In doing so, we consider what insights each framework may provide for the design and implementation of future climate activism and civil resistance.

Chapter 6 closes the monograph with a summary of lessons drawn from this empirical analysis which may be useful to academics and movement activists and organizers.

# Chapter 1: The Emergence of Civil Resistance Against Climate Change

## Climate Change as a Global Issue

The potential for humanity to alter the climate on a global scale has been known for many decades. From early hypotheses linking increased carbon dioxide and a warming climate in the late 1930s (Callendar 1938) to the 2018 IPCC report giving only 12 years to reach a pathway to net zero emissions by 2050, countless warnings have been given of the urgent need to reduce carbon dioxide and other greenhouse gas emissions. The consequences of ignoring these calls are abundantly clear. Increased glacial melting and sea level rise, extreme weather, and migration and extinction of numerous animal and plant species are predicted with high confidence. Impacts will be disproportionately experienced by the world's poorest people, with risks of flooding, food shortages, and sea level rise spreading across South Asia, sub-Saharan Africa, the Middle East, and East Asia (IPCC 2018). Human health impacts include increased injuries, disease, and death due to heatwaves, reduced air quality, and increased animal-borne diseases. Other climate change effects on tourism, transportation, and energy systems will likely act as multipliers, increasing poverty and disadvantage in communities around the globe. Indeed, agencies as diverse as the Pentagon (the US military) and European Council (heads of the European Union states) see climate change as not just an environmental or humanitarian issue, but as a threat to collective international security (Dawson 2010). Yet national governments, with very few exceptions, have not adequately responded to this challenge. And as the reports have multiplied and calls for proportionate political responses have intensified, a growing movement of activists has emerged to demand effective action.

## The Emergence of Civil Resistance Against Climate Change

Civil resistance against climate change has deep roots in the past mobilization of movements for social justice, democracy, and sustainability. It builds on a history of environmental collective action emerging from concerns around issues such as wildlife preservation, clean water infrastructure, and the impact of toxins and pollutants. Over the last fifty years, in particular, activists have begun to draw connections between environmental problems and issues related to power and wealth inequities, industrialization, and colonization (Lander et al. 2009). In the United States, struggles against waste dumping, racial disparities in public health risks, and ecological injustices committed in communities of color helped to formulate environmental justice as an overarching frame for environmental activism. Activists used the lessons learned from the civil rights movement to more effectively frame their issues and mobilize supporters (McCright and Dunlap 2008).

In the 1980s, organizers developed a range of climate networks, such as the Climate Action Network, which formed in 1989. These networks linked activists across international borders and ushered in a range of new activities, such as appeals for action on climate change by Nobel Prize winners and members of the US National Academy of Science in 1987. In following decades, a vibrant mix of actors emerged who used diverse tactics with sometimes disparate social and political visions (De Lucia 2014), from large transnational organizations such as 350.org to loose, informal networks such as Rising Tide. The targets of climate activism are also diverse, with grassroots organizations such as the Tar Sands Blockade focusing on fossil fuel projects and power plants, and formal networks such as the Philippines Movement for Climate Justice (a network of over 100 organizations) and Climate Justice Now (CJN) including Indigenous peoples and immigrant workers (Smith and Patterson 2019). This range of actors is noticeable at gatherings such as the Copenhagen Conference of Parties 2015 summit, which included a huge range of civil society actors: direct action networks, grassroots social movements from the global south, non-governmental organizations (NGOs), trade unions, journalists, individuals, and politicians (Chatterton, Featherstone, and Routledge 2013).

Some of the earliest identified climate-related civil resistance actions to have occurred date from 2002, when Greenpeace activists shut down Esso gas stations in Luxembourg (Brecher 2015). Over the following decade actions against diverse targets flourished. Protests against mountain top removal coal mining in the United States began in 2005, "climate camps" combining eco-loving workshops with trespass and squatting began in 2006, and further protests against coal mining began spreading in many countries. The emergence of a new organization named 350.org more clearly linked climate activism with civil resistance, most particularly during two global actions against fossil fuel industries. The first 2009 Global Day of Action resulted in more than 2,500 actions in 181 countries (White 2009), and the second 2016 "Break Free" actions spread across six continents, including Australia, where over 2,000 individuals blockaded the country's largest coal port. Over the next few years, resistance activity continued. These included the establishment of forums such as the Climate Justice Summit in 2000, the international Peoples' March against climate change in 2009, the Global Climate March in 2015, and a range of conferences such as "Power Shift" and the "World People's Conference of Climate Change and the Rights of Mother Earth" (Chatterton, et al. 2013). At the same time, groups and networks such as Transition Towns and the Global Ecovillage Network focused on building community self-reliance and climate resilience (Barr and Pollard 2017).

Although there had been decades of mobilization on a variety of environmental issues, when Sharp wrote his seminal categorization of nonviolent tactics in 1973 there was no climate movement nor any widespread shared concern around climate issues expressed through civil resistance. As Beer (2021) has highlighted in his updated list of civil resistance methods, and as we see through this short timeline of civil resistance against climate change, tactics have evolved since the 1970s and continue to develop. For example, more recent forms of nonviolent tactics include the use of online disruption—such as denial of service attacks or online posting of recordings of police brutality against activists—that capitalize on the opportunities and weaknesses of social media technologies. Consumer boycotts of products and queue-ins at businesses suggest increased targeting of the corporate sector in addition to government and political entities. Street theatre such as die-ins and Extinction Rebellion's Red Rebels has created evocative imagery as well as increased modes of engagement. In addition, practitioners and scholars such as Bill Moyer (2001) have highlighted how these tactics may differ across different groups, with some groups and individuals more open to including civil resistance or even violent tactics such as property destruction in their repertoire, as opposed to conventional tactics. To help make sense of what the range of tactics may mean for the future of the climate movement, we now turn to the scholarship of movement frameworks.

## Movement Frameworks

Why do some movements grow and build power, while others shrink and eventually dissipate? There is a large body of literature crossing multiple research fields looking into the factors that influence social movement mobilization and the achievement of movement goals. Civil resistance against climate change occurs within the wider context of the environmental movement, with evidence demonstrating that many groups focus on both climate change and other environmental issues, while also engaging in both conventional and civil resistance tactics (Gulliver, Fielding, and Louis 2020). There is currently no integrative framework enabling an empirical analysis of the characteristics and outcomes of civil resistance against climate change. This study applies empirical data to existing frameworks to identify the extent to which they map onto the climate change civil resistance movement. In addition, it seeks to apply these existing frameworks to better understand whether civil resistance against climate change has the potential to achieve success.

In this section we provide a brief overview of three frameworks constructed to help explain the emergence and progression of social movements. The three frameworks we consider are the "Great Turning" (Macy 2007), the "Climate Insurgency" (Brecher 2015), and the political process model (McAdam 1982; Tilly 1978). The first two frameworks were chosen because they were created specifically to chart the progression of environmental and climate movements. The third framework has been widely used in the analysis of a range of environmental and social movements. It highlights key political, communication, and organizational characteristics which affect movement progression. Each framework identifies different components which may be important for increasing the likelihood that tactics will be successful. Mapping empirical data against each of these components will help to identify which frameworks offer insight for climate activists seeking to increase their opportunities to achieve success. It may also help inform the development of an integrative framework specifically tracking the development of climate change activism.

In the following sections we present the key components in each of these frameworks and the data we will use to map each component. We then present and interpret the data in Chapters 2 through 4. Finally, in Chapter 5 we map our data against these frameworks to identify any insights that can guide the design of more effective mobilization.

**Great Turning Model**

Joanna Macy's (2007) Great Turning presents a model of three mutually reinforcing dimensions of change: the first dimension relates to undertaking actions aimed at slowing down environmental destruction, the second dimension to shifting consciousness and values at an individual level, and the third dimension to building alternative structures (see Figure 1).

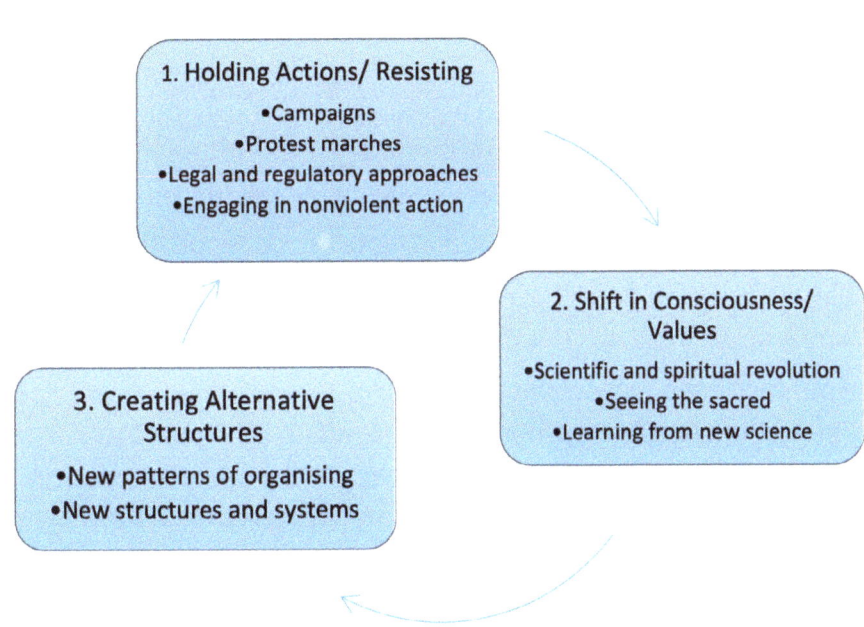

FIGURE 1. Three Components of the Great Turning (Macy 2007)

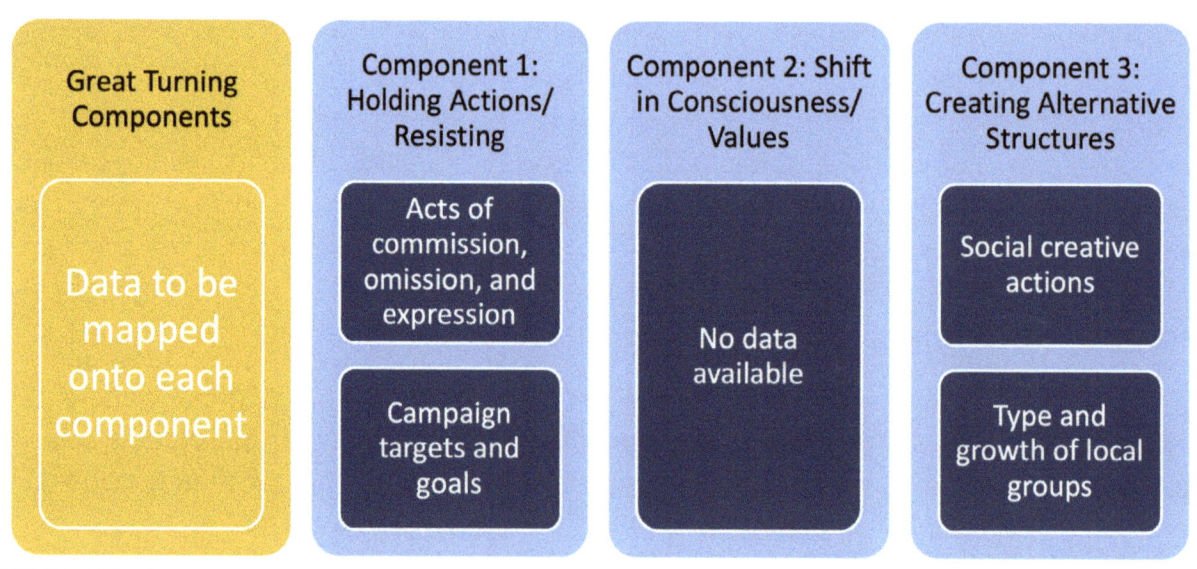

FIGURE 2. Great Turning Components and Data to Be Mapped onto Each Component

For Macy, the actions that must occur in Component 1 to slow the pace of environmental destruction include engaging in civil resistance tactics and other forms of activism. Although most of these activities align with Beer's (2021) categorization of disruptive civil resistance, this component also includes tactics such as engaging in legal challenges and demanding regulatory protection for the environment, which are not included in Beer's categorization as a nonviolent resistance action due to their use of institutional channels. As such, in order to assess the degree to which the climate movement is undertaking actions that reflect Macy's first component (i.e., holding actions/resisting), we consider the full range of civil resistance tactics, and more specifically the proportion and type of acts of commission, omission, and expression used by climate change groups. We also assess the degree to which climate change campaigns have legal or regulatory goals that align with Component 1.

Component 2 of the model argues that a society-wide change in consciousness and values is required to successfully address our environmental problems. While we are not able to directly measure Macy's second component—the degree to which there has been a mass change of values—there is other research demonstrating a shift in societal values relating to the environment (Lampert, Metaal, Liu, and Gambarin 2019). We return to this point in Chapter 6.

Finally, Macy argues in Component 3 that there is also a need for a simultaneous grassroots process of reinvention of the way that we live. This can occur both through personal choices about how to live and through shaping a new sustainable economy and society. As these types of actions align with Beer's social creative nonviolent actions, we consider the proportion and type of social creative actions used by climate change groups to map onto this component. In addition, Macy highlights the need for groups to work together to create alternative systems and structures such as eco-villages, renewable energy cooperatives, and community gardens (Power 2015). To identify whether this is occurring, we consider the extent to which these types of local groups are appearing in our data. Figure 2 highlights each component of the Great Turning and the data that we present in the following chapters to map onto those components.

**Climate Insurgency Model**

The two components of holding actions and creating alternative structures are also found in Jeremy Brecher's (2009) Climate Insurgency model. Brecher argues that the movement must engage in an "insurgency of nonviolent action." By insurgency he means a rapid, mass engagement in nonviolent action challenging the legitimacy of existing state and corporate authority. Brecher argues that this is required because the established authority has both caused and perpetuated the systems and behaviors that drive climate change. In order to identify the extent to which the Australian climate change civil resistance movement reflects Brecher's call to insurgency, we will present data on the type and frequency of civil resistance occurring in the movement.

Second, Brecher argues that the movement must be built on two processes to achieve the change needed to address climate change: self-organization and deisolation. Self-organization refers to the ability of individuals to organize themselves into mobilizing structures in their local communities. Although Brecher does not argue that these mobilizing structures need to create alternative systems such as localized food production networks or renewable energy projects (as argued in the Great Turning model), he does stress the importance of local groups and localized action in driving urgent action on climate. For Brecher, these localized groups are important because it is through these groups that individuals will build bonds of trust, which will then support mobilization in local communities at the scale required for an insurgency. The second process is deisolation, which has two dimensions: first, individuals meeting like-minded people through these local groups, and second, the framing of climate action to change the systems that entrench climate destruction instead of merely changing personal behaviors such as recycling plastics or reducing car use. Brecher argues these measures are insufficient for addressing the climate crisis and that, instead, the systems that perpetuate climate-destructive practices—such as the proliferation of plastic packaging and dependency on fossil fuel consumption—must be urgently changed.

We consider the extent to which the second component of the Climate Insurgency model of self-organization and deisolation is occurring in the climate change movement in Australia by looking at data on the growth of local climate action groups. We also consider the goals and targets of climate change campaigns to ascertain whether these campaigns are directed at individual carbon reduction behaviors (such as increased public transport usage) or the

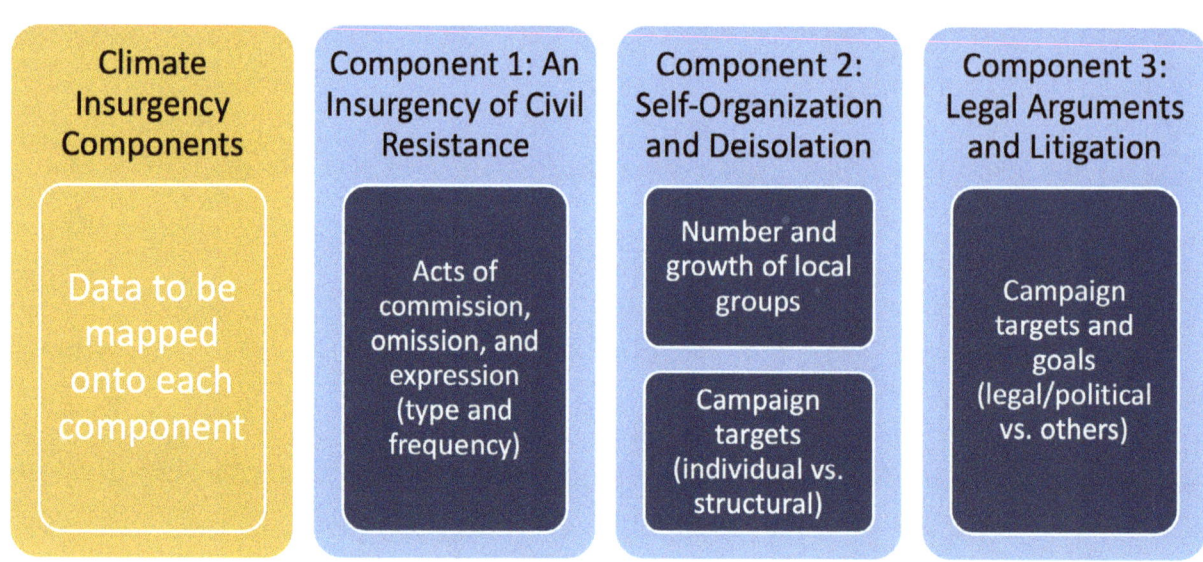

FIGURE 3. Climate Insurgency Components and Data to Be Mapped onto Each Component

systems and structures propping up continued carbon emissions (such as policies supporting increased fossil fuel production and consumption).

The third component of the Climate Insurgency model focuses on legal arguments and litigation. Brecher argues that litigation challenging the legitimacy of insufficient state responses to climate degradation is a critical factor forcing governments to prioritize urgent and effective responses to climate change. We consider the extent to which litigation has been used in the Australian climate movement to identify whether this component holds potential to drive change in the Australian context. Figure 3 presents the three components of the Climate Insurgency model and the data we present in subsequent chapters that maps onto each component.

**The Political Process Model**

The Political Process model identifies three components that help explain how movements emerge and achieve success: their opportunity to engage in the political process, their mobilizing structures, and the way they frame their concerns. The first of these components—political opportunities—reflects the particular power relations that movements face at any one time. Polletta (2008) identifies three key features of the successful use of political opportunities: being heard in the political arena, capitalizing on political changes, and finding new allies. The first of these is important because groups within movements often lack access or standing in institutional politics, limiting their ability to drive change using conventional channels. McAdam (2017), in his study of climate activism in the United States, demonstrates how this power matters in his analysis of climate groups. He argues that their opportunities were constrained by the dominance of the Republican Party, the barriers presented by partisan polarization, and the influence of Big Oil and money in politics. These barriers reduced the effectiveness of climate change groups to achieve their goals. Whether groups are able to effectively respond to changes in political circumstances—whether national or international—and find new allies to help build power for their cause also impacts their ability to achieve their goals. This is because changes in political circumstances—such as economic crises, war, or regime changes—can all affect the degree to which groups are able to gain access to, and engage with, the political process. To assess whether Australian climate change groups are capitalizing on the political opportunities available to them, we consider the outcomes of campaigns targeting political entities and whether groups are finding new allies to help further their cause.

The second component of the political process model is "mobilizing structures." These structures are the collective vehicles through which individuals are connected and mobilized into action (McAdam 2017). Structures can refer to organizational type (e.g., grassroots versus large professional or not-for-profit organizations), the networks linking individual groups, and material resources such as money and volunteers (McAdam, McCarthy, and Zald 1996; McCarthy and Zald 1977). A large body of research has argued that the existence of established movement groups with greater resources will facilitate the emergence of a social movement (McAdam 1999), and the resources they acquire will impact the success of their activities (Andrews and Edwards 2004). Of particular interest is the debate around whether large, well-funded and well-staffed organizations may effectively mobilize large numbers of supporters (Richards and Heard 2005).

However, some researchers argue that the long-term success of movements is instead dependent on mobilizing structures built on a foundation of grassroots organizations and informal networks (McAdam 2017). Grassroots groups may be able to participate in a greater range of civil resistance actions as opposed to more formal NGOs that rely on stable funding streams and long-term engagement in formal political processes, which constrains their tactical choices (Zchout and Tal 2017). To be successful, these grassroots groups need to be able to engage in sustained civil resistance, support leaders able to organize these actions (Ganz 2010), and pursue multiple goals (Polletta 2008). Thus, effective mobilizing structures may have three characteristics which we consider in this monograph: grassroots groups, a range of informal networks, and the ability to sustain civil resistance with multiple goals.

The third component of the political process model relates to how movements frame their issues. Framing was identified by Benford and Snow (2000) as a central dynamic in understanding how social movements motivate participants and legitimize their struggle (Moser 2007). Framing issues helps catalyze mobilization by conveying a shared sense of grievance about the climate issue, alongside a belief that acting collectively will help solve the problem (McAdam 2017).

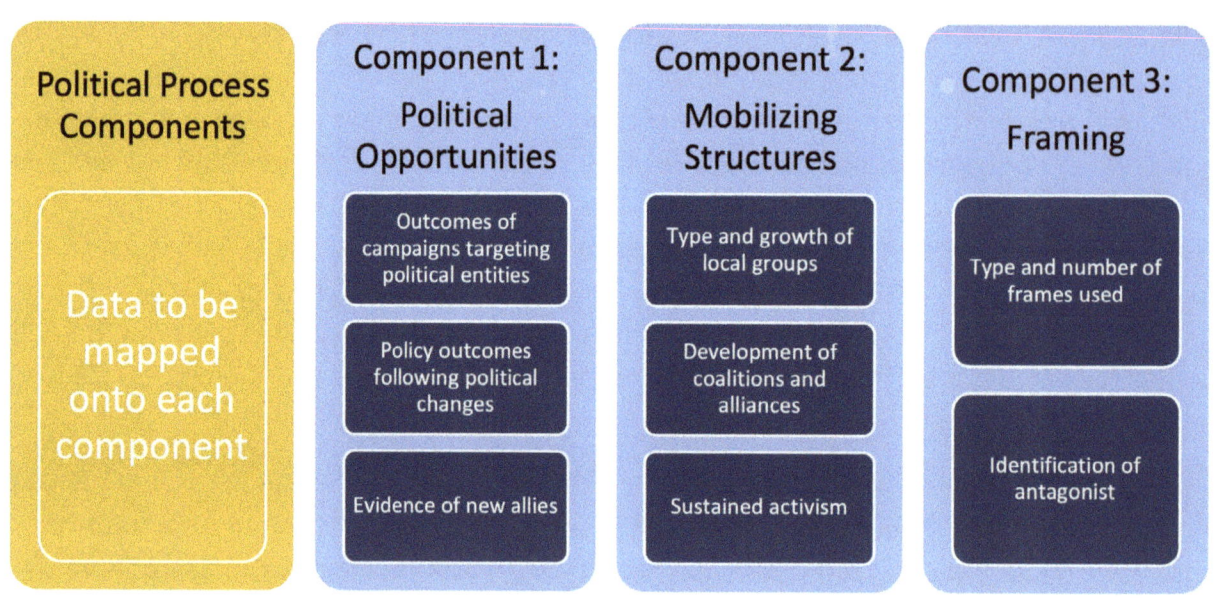

FIGURE 4. Political Process Model Components and Data to Be Mapped onto Each Component

We consider three aspects of framing using our dataset. First, effective framing needs to highlight the issue of climate change and offer solutions. It should also identify an antagonist (Polletta 2008). This is a challenge for the climate change movement, which has also been framed as a lifestyle movement rather than one demanding changes to political and economic systems (Polletta 2008). Second, given that some frames may be effective at mobilizing supporters but ineffective at persuading policymakers (Amenta 2008), some researchers have argued that movements maximize their ability to effectively communicate their concerns when using multiple frames (Polletta 2008). This is particularly important given that some climate change frames used in the past—such as "scientific uncertainty," "negative economic consequences" of climate change action, and "climate crisis,"—have played a role in reinforcing partisan divides (Nisbet 2009). Multiple frames can instead provide an opportunity to link climate messages with an audience's preexisting values and worldview. Although framing processes are usually investigated through content analysis of text, we instead use automated text analysis tools to consider how climate change groups frame the issue of climate change. This approach enables us to examine a very large collection of over 65,000 pages of website text. We also investigate the targets of climate change campaigns to ascertain whether groups identify antagonists in their framing.

The Political Process model is nuanced and involves multiple questions across these three components. Figure 4 highlights the data sets we draw on in order to map this model against the climate change civil resistance movement in Australia.

## Summary

This chapter has provided a brief overview of the emergence of civil resistance against climate change and has presented three key frameworks to help us track the progression of the climate movement. Across these three frameworks we have identified nine components, of which eight can be applied to the data collected on the Australian environmental movement. Through mapping the data onto these eight components, we identify the extent to which this movement leads positive environmental change by a) selecting effective tactics, (b) uniting in appropriate organizational structures, (c) capitalizing on opportunities to create change, and (d) framing messages which draw attention to the issue and build support for their cause.

Both the Great Turning and the Climate Insurgency models highlight the importance of tactical choice and local mobilization. As such, we use Beer's (2021) categorization of civil resistance tactics as a mechanism to identify what tactics are used by the movement and the extent to which local grassroots groups are creating alternative structures through using social creative actions (Component 3 of the Great Turning). We also consider organizational structures to investigate the extent to which environmental groups are self-organizing (Component 2 of the Climate Insurgency model) and building networks to drive and sustain their efforts (Component 2 of the Political Process model). We then consider the characteristics and outcomes of climate change campaigns, first to assess the extent to which the climate movement is using legal means to effect change (Component 3 of the Climate Insurgency model), and second to examine whether the climate change movement is capitalizing on political opportunities in the Australian context (Component 1 of the Political Process model). Finally, we consider how environmental groups are framing their communication about climate change (Component 3 of the Political Process model).

In Chapter 2, we use a large body of data collected on the Australian environmental movement to undertake this mapping process. We present data on the tactics, groups, communication framing, campaigns, and campaign outcomes present in the movement, as well as the range of tactics used that map onto Beer's (2021) civil resistance categorizations. We then consider two campaigns in detail in Chapters 3 and 4 and focus specifically on the extent to which civil resistance against climate change in Australia is attracting repressive state responses in Chapter 5. In our final Chapter we gather the insights from these four empirical chapters to consider the extent to which climate change civil resistance in Australia maps onto these frameworks. Our aim is that this work identifies components most valuable for future empirical analysis, which can then inform the future development of an integrative theoretical model of climate change activism. In doing so, we also shed light on the extent to which the movement is capitalizing on the opportunities it must create to sustain meaningful action against climate change.

# Chapter 2: The Australian Climate Change Civil Resistance Movement

Climate change civil resistance does not occur in a vacuum. Groups advocating for action against climate change exist within a wider environmental movement and may engage in a diverse repertoire of action, encompassing both conventional and civil resistance tactics. To better understand the characteristics of climate change civil resistance, we begin by presenting information on a broad range of groups involved in environmental activism in Australia. We then delve more deeply into climate change-related civil resistance tactics and campaigns. Figure 5 provides an overview of the data presented in this chapter.

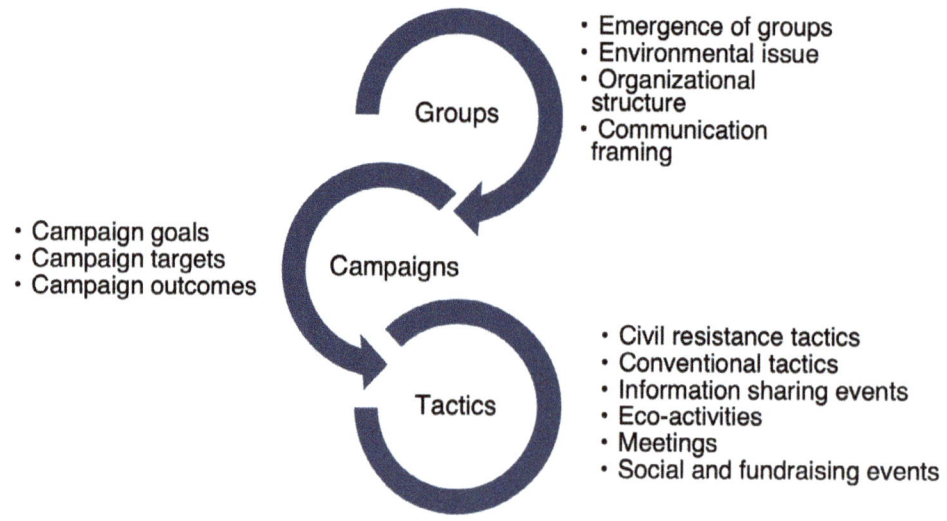

**FIGURE 5.** Information Presented in This Chapter

By beginning with an overview of Australian environmental activism, we hope that scholars and activists can use this process as a reference point to map the full range of groups and activities of environmental movements within their own countries. This approach also enables scholars and activists to identify links between civil resistance and the wider environmental movement. We trust that this data can be used as a stimulus to reflect on whether other national and local environmental movements are successfully mobilizing their communities and achieving positive environmental change, both to address the climate crisis and the wider environmental problems we face globally.

## The Australian Context

Over the last few decades, Australia has begun to experience the impacts of climate change, with many signs pointing to an increasing range and number of negative effects. For example, the millennium drought from 2001 to 2009 resulted in severe ecological damage to extensive river systems, causing a water crisis in most Australian cities and a major reduction in agricultural production (Van Dijk et al. 2013). Catastrophic forest fires or "bushfires" in recent summer seasons—most particularly in 2009 and the 2019–20 season—are associated with the changing climate. These effects have led to the destruction of entire ecological systems and have caused substantial loss of human life and economic damage (United Nations 2020). However, not only is Australia vulnerable to climate change impacts such as drought, fire, sea level rise, and endemic species extinctions, it also has a strong tradition of skepticism and doubt toward the need to take climate change action. It is thus unsurprising that Australia has been called "climate change ground zero," both in terms of suffering the effects of climate change but also in terms of sustaining entrenched climate policy uncertainty (Laureates Open Letter 2020).

This skepticism and doubt have resulted from and contributed to the so-called "climate wars" between the major political parties during the past decade (Baker 2020). Emissions trading schemes have been proposed and shelved, a carbon pricing scheme legislated and removed, and the issue of climate change itself has destabilized and deposed prime ministers (Beeson and McDonald 2013). Moreover, years of media coverage regarding inadequate political responses to the threat of climate change appears not to have resulted in meaningful cultural or political change. Indeed, the Climate Action Tracker website—which tracks international progress toward remaining under the 2°C warming threshold—highlights a body of evidence demonstrating the insufficient responses currently made by the Australian government. These include the dismissal of the IPCC Special Report *Global Warming of 1.5°C*, halting funding for the Green Climate Fund, continued support for the ineffective Climate Solutions Fund policy instrument, ramping up liquefied natural gas exports, and ignoring calls from Australian residents and Pacific Island neighbors to enact meaningful emissions reductions strategies (Climate Action Tracker 2020).

During these years of policy struggle, a vibrant and growing network of climate activists has emerged. This civil sector response has focused on key themes of demanding effective climate policy, halting the expansion of fossil fuel dependence, and supporting increased renewable energy (Pearse 2016). These demands were accelerated with a surge in the development of local climate action groups and the parallel growth of groups establishing alternative local sustainable systems such as "transition towns" and sustainable living collectives (Gulliver et al. 2020). Compared to other countries (see Dawson 2010; Kössler 2014), there has been comparatively little focus on "climate justice" in Australia, although the term is just now being used, as we highlight below. In this chapter we investigate how the environmental movement has emerged in the years 2010–2020, the characteristics of groups active in the movement, and the campaigns and tactics they are engaged in. We start by outlining our methodology and data collection efforts and analysis.

## Data Collection, Methodology, and Analysis

As discussed in earlier sections, climate change groups engaged in civil resistance operate within the larger environmental movement. Through an online database search in 2020, we built a dataset comprised of 492 groups which specified in their website text that they were engaged in environmental activism on one or more environmental issues.[3]

This dataset has four components: first, data collected includes website content from the 492 groups; second, external online content collected on the outcomes of 193 climate change campaigns; and third, organizational data acquired from the Australian Charities and Not-for-profits Commission (ACNC). The fourth component of the dataset records every event promoted by groups via their Facebook pages between 2010 and 2020. The 492 groups had a total of 728 Facebook pages. While some groups have only one (or no) Facebook page, some organizations have local branches or sub-groups with their own page. Across these 728 Facebook pages, 36,541 events were promoted, of which 8,607 were duplicate events. Duplicate events occur when groups use the "cohosting" option available on Facebook to share amongst their own supporters. After removing duplicates, we were able to analyze a total of 27,934 unique events.

A range of tools were then used to analyze each of the four components of this dataset. First, website content was manually coded to identify the focal issue of each environmental group, their year of formation, and the campaigns they were undertaking. A search of each group in online databases for charities and businesses enabled the identification of the legal organizational status of each group. Second, we looked at how groups were communicating their issues by undertaking topic modeling using the R "Topicmodel" package (Grün and Hornik 2011). This algorithm identified the key topics and terms used in the language on the groups' websites. We then investigated the 27,934 unique events organized by these groups. As we wish to understand the type and proportion of civil resistance tactics that the groups used, we began by assembling events into five distinct categories (see Table 3).

Using an Excel macro, events were categorized into types by the event title. For example, 1,622 events had the words "film," "movie," or "screening" in their title and were categorized as "film screenings." Each of these event types was then grouped into one of the five

---

3   The full methodology details are available in the Appendix.

overarching categories shown in Table 3. Following this, the civil resistance actions were then manually reviewed and matched against Beer's (2021) typology of nonviolent action, as shown in Table 1.

### Table 3. Event Categories, Descriptions, and Examples

| EVENT GROUP | DESCRIPTION | EXAMPLES |
|---|---|---|
| Information sharing activities | These are events where the main goal is to provide information to participants about a particular issue or topic | Film screenings<br>Book discussions<br>Candidate forums |
| Eco-activities | These events involve a hands-on component with an environmental purpose | Rubbish clean-up activities<br>Permaculture workshops<br>Tree planting activities |
| Meetings and administration events | These events involve bringing individuals together to undertake planning or regular meetings | Campaign catch up<br>Annual general meeting (AGM)<br>Working group meeting |
| Social and fundraising events | These events can be those organized purely for socializing with other group members or for fundraising for group or campaign activities | Christmas party<br>Comedy night<br>Fundraising gig<br>Games night |
| Civil resistance tactics | These events include those related to civil resistance tactics, namely acts of commission, omission, and expression. | Rally<br>Climate strike<br>Blockade |

Finally, the chapter reports on climate change campaign outcomes. In total, 906 campaigns were identified through an analysis of the website text of the 492 groups. Of these, 193 campaigns focused on an issue related to climate change. Each campaign was reviewed to identify the campaign goal and target. An online search for campaign outcomes was then completed to identify which climate campaigns had achieved success. Although we are able through this approach to identify which goals had been achieved, the limitations of the data mean that we are unable to state whether it was the activities of the group or campaign that caused a particular outcome.

This extensive and mixed methods data collection and analysis has a range of benefits. Given that groups involved in social and environmental activism are increasingly using online communication (Schäfer 2012), using these channels to collect data offers unprecedented insight into their activities and the way they frame environmental issues. Through collecting data on their online content, we can both gather key information on group characteristics—including grassroots groups which may not exist in any government databases—and investigate how groups are communicating about their activities to the general public. In addition, modern tools such as R (R Core Team 2013) enable the analysis of big datasets such as these to provide additional insights about patterns and trends. Using an extensive range of analysis tools allows us to better understand the nature of climate change activism and to study the characteristics and activities of the groups involved in climate change civil resistance.

## Climate Change Activism Within the Australian Environmental Movement

We begin this section by considering groups involved in general environmental activism before focusing in more detail on groups focused on climate change and civil resistance tactics. In this section we look at the historical development of groups over time as well as the number of groups and their organizational status. We also examine how they are framing environmental and climate change issues through text analysis of their website content. We then take a detailed look at the type of events, and specifically, the civil resistance tactics occurring across the movement (e.g., rallies, blockades). Finally, we present data on climate change campaigns and their outcomes. We close the chapter with a discussion of key findings.

### The Emergence of Environmental and Climate Change Groups

By analyzing each group's website text, we gathered information on the date on which they began their work and their primary environmental focus. Of the 492 groups, 320 listed the year they were founded. Since most groups focused on a range of issues, we categorized them according to the primary environmental issue of focus as stated on their websites, which were then grouped into eight main issues (see the Appendix for details).

The majority of groups were focused on conservation and protection issues, such as flora and fauna protection ($n = 254$, 51%). A total of 153 groups in our dataset (31%) work in four areas directly related to climate change: sustainability, mining, renewable energy, and climate. These groups work to address either the causes of climate change (e.g., stopping new fossil fuel mines) or to develop solutions to reduce climate change (e.g., the development of sustainable food or renewable energy systems). This contrasts with groups focusing on pollution (e.g., landfill remediation, pesticides and water pollution) and waste (e.g., plastic bag bans, ocean cleanups). Although these latter groups may invoke climate change as one of the reasons for their activism, they do not list climate change as their primary focus on their websites.

Figure 6 shows that the focus on climate change is a relatively new phenomenon in the Australian environmental movement. Environmental groups in Australia from 1883 to around 2005 focused on the issues of conservation, waste, pollution, and nuclear waste. The earliest predecessor of climate-focused groups are those that were active in sustainability. For example, Friends of the Earth was founded in 1974, describing itself as a sustainability group, while Sustainable Living Tasmania was founded in 1972. While these groups describe themselves as focused on sustainability, they often also campaign on other issues such as mining and conservation.

From 2006 onward, a wave of new groups dedicated primarily to climate change were formed, alongside groups focusing primarily on opposition to mining (such as coal seam gas mining). In addition, groups focusing on renewable energy emerged, working primarily on initiating community-owned renewable energy projects and fostering sustainable communities.

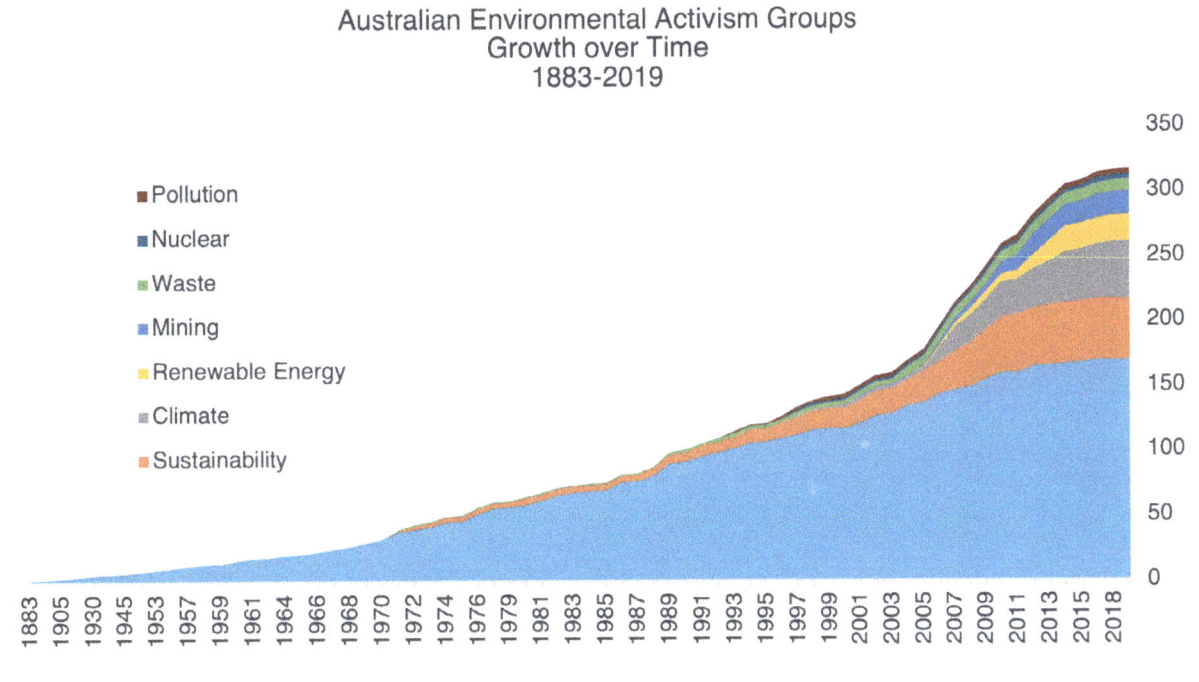

FIGURE 6. Emergence of Environmental Activism Groups in Australia

Despite this growth, however, we also found that groups may reduce their activity over time. Of the 492 groups analyzed, 129 had not updated their website for more than 365 days. Although we are unable to assess whether these groups remain active, this information indicates that some groups at least may decrease activity or completely disband over time.

**Organizational Structures**

Some scholars have argued that more formal organizational structures influence tactical choice; when organizations have staff to pay and grants to acquire, their engagement in civil resistance tactics may decrease (McAdam 1982). In Australia a range of organizational types are possible. Groups engaging in activism can have a formal legal structure (such as a company or an incorporated association) and can apply for charitable status. Alternatively, they can operate without any legally recognized or formal status. Table 4 (on the following page) shows these three overarching options (organizations with charitable status, organizations without charitable status, and groups with no formal status) along with their key characteristics, descriptions, and the organizational status of the 728 Facebook pages belonging to the 492 environmental groups.

As the right-hand column of Table 4 shows, 305 groups have no formal charitable or incorporated/company status. Given that companies and groups with charitable status are restricted from engaging in illegal activities, a lack of formal status enables groups to support or engage in illegal activities (so far as any individual citizen is able). Groups supporting and conducting acts of civil disobedience—such as 350.org's promotion of a blockade of the Newcastle Coal Port—have faced legal challenges to remove their charitable status and restrict their activities. Thus, operating without legal status can provide groups with freedom of choice regarding the tactics they engage in.

Table 4. Organizational Status of Environmental Groups and Sub-Groups

| ORGANIZATIONAL STATUS* | N | WITH CHARITABLE STATUS | | | WITHOUT CHARITABLE STATUS | | NO FORMAL STATUS |
|---|---|---|---|---|---|---|---|
| | | DGR Status** | Company | Incorporated Association | Incorporated Association | Company | |
| Tax refund for donations over AU$2 | | ✓ | x | x | x | x | x |
| Access to tax concessions and other concessions/exemptions | | ✓ | ✓ | ✓ | x | x | x |
| Receive and spend financial resources | | ✓ | ✓ | ✓ | ✓ | ✓ | x |
| Required to file records with federal/state governments | | ✓ | ✓ | ✓ | ✓ | ✓ | x |
| Individuals are personally liable for claims | | x | x | x | x | x | ✓ |
| Advocate direct action[4] | | x | x | x | x | x | ✓ |
| Promote or oppose a political party or candidate | | x | x | x | x | x | ✓ |
| Environmental umbrella groups | 263 | 86 | 3 | 120 | 59 | 9 | 72 |
| Environmental sub-groups | 83 | 53 | - | 71 | - | 4 | 8 |
| Climate change umbrella groups | 183 | 20 | 2 | 34 | 34 | 8 | 105 |
| Climate change sub-groups | 199 | 52 | - | 53 | - | 26 | 120 |
| Total | 728 | 211 | 5 | 278 | 93 | 47 | 305 |

\* Note: This table is a simplified overview of the complex legislation surrounding not-for-profit organizational status in Australia. Each criterion is therefore subject to caveats in practice.

\*\* DGR: Deductible Gift Recipient status. Entities with DGR status can receive tax deductible gifts.

However, there are also considerable risks to groups engaging in activism without formal status under Australian law. These groups may struggle to acquire and manage financial resources (unless individuals acquire it on their behalf), they are unable to apply for grants or pay staff, and they also face increased personal liability for any negative outcomes such as property damage or personal injury.[5] Thus, groups must weigh a difficult decision whether to obtain formal organizational status.

---

4   In Australia, advocating illegal activities or engaging in political electioneering is prohibited for organizations with charitable status. The Australian Federal Government has, for example, denied charitable status registration to Greenpeace in 2018 (Murray 2019), and undertaken sustained efforts to achieve electoral legislation reform, investigate environmental organizations, and question the ACNC regarding charity electioneering (Murray, 2019).

5   See **ourcommunity.com.au** for more information regarding personal liability.

Table 4 shows that the majority of informal groups (225 out of 305) are focused on climate change. A total of 105 of these act as umbrella groups (e.g., Stop Adani) with 120 sub-groups (e.g., Stop Adani Brisbane) between them. This suggests that the climate change movement is emerging through grassroots structures without formal organizational status and is connected through networks of umbrella and sub-groups. This may be beneficial in that it eliminates the need for burdensome administration and reporting (required by groups with formal organizational status). The interconnected structure of many of these grassroots groups may also encourage sharing campaign design and implementation tasks, whereas independent groups with formal organizational status may require proprietary or branded materials.

**Framing of Environmental and Climate Issues**

In order to identify how groups are framing the environmental issues for which they advocate, we investigated the language used in their website communication. We used Linguistic Inquiry and Word Count automated software (LIWC: Pennebaker, Boyd, Jordan, and Blackburn 2015) to search through the full text of each website (where text was able to be scraped) to identify how climate, justice, conservation, and sustainability issues are framed. This software identifies the proportion of those words found across the full text dataset and delivers the result as a percentage of the total word count (i.e., that the word "climate" makes up 1.21% of the words used on the websites of climate change-focused groups). This enables an overview of word frequency which can help identify whether environmental groups with different primary environmental foci frame their environmental issues differently.

While we focus on these four words in this section, we suggest that other environmental and justice related terms such as "Indigenous rights" could be considered for future detailed analysis of word frequency across the dataset. Table 5 presents the results.

### Table 5. Frequency of Words Related to Climate, Justice, Conservation, and Sustainability Occurring on Environmental Group Websites

| PRIMARY ENVIRONMENTAL ISSUE | NUMBER OF GROUPS | FREQUENCY OF USE OF WORDS | | | |
|---|---|---|---|---|---|
| | | Climate | Justice | Conservation | Sustainability |
| Climate | 83 | 1.21% | 0.01% | 0.04% | 0.20% |
| Mining | 37 | 0.09% | 0.00% | 0.03% | 0.04% |
| Renewable energy | 32 | 0.12% | 0.00% | 0.03% | 0.17% |
| Sustainability | 64 | 0.18% | 0.01% | 0.05% | 0.53% |
| Conservation, waste, nuclear & pollution | 276 | 0.05% | 0.01% | 0.12% | 0.09% |
| Average | 492 | 0.33% | 0.01% | 0.06% | 0.21% |

Table 5 indicates that the word "climate" was used more frequently in climate change-focused groups, as was "conservation" in conservation groups. The word "sustainability" was used frequently across all groups, excluding those focused on mining. The word "justice" was rarely used but did occur at low frequencies on the websites of groups focusing on climate.

Topic modeling using R Topic Models package (Grün and Hornik 2011) was then undertaken to identify what words across all 492 websites co-occurred the most frequently with the word "climate." Topic Models software uses Latent Dirichlet Allocation (LDA), a mathematical process that treats each document as a mixture of topics, and each topic as a mixture of words. We used this method to detect the co-occurrence of the word "climate" with four different sets of words (listed in the "Words" column in Table 6). In addition, this algorithm counts the number of websites focusing on each of the four topics. These four climate topics appeared as the most common environmental topic in 114 of the 492 websites (23%), with words connected to mining found in two of the four topics.

### Table 6. Climate Change Topics and Most Frequent Words in Environmental Group Websites

| TOPIC | WORDS | NUMBER OF WEBSITES WITH TOPIC CO-OCCURRENCE |
|---|---|---|
| Climate + mine | Mine, community, campaign, coal, Australia, nuclear, action, water, people, support, energy | 86 (17%) |
| Climate + health | Protect, health, report, Queensland, member, donate, change, nation, policy, media, submission | 16 (3%) |
| Climate + finance | Coal, Australia, fossil, company, fuel, fund, super, invest, Adani, change, global | 7 (1%) |
| Climate + reef | Cairns, event, reef, donate, develop, plastic, sustain, mangrove, dredge, community, clean | 5 (1%) |
| Total | | 114 (23%) |

Figure 7 visualizes how environmental groups in Australia are framing the issue of climate change on their websites.[6] This word cloud presents the 35 most common words associated with climate change across the four topics identified in Table 6.

The size of the words indicates their prevalence within the four topics. Across all topics the most common words associated with climate change were "donate" and "energy."

---

6   This word cloud was generated by the authors using **www.wordart.com**.

**FIGURE 7.** Words Most Commonly Associated with Climate Topics in Environmental Group Websites

**Events and Civil Resistance Tactics**

In this section we present information on the range of activities undertaken by the 492 Australian environmental groups and their 728 associated Facebook pages. As highlighted earlier, many environmental groups have "sub-groups," that is, groups that are local branches or offshoots of an organization (see Figure 8 on the following page). An example of this is the National Park Association of Australia. This group has one overarching national organization and nine state or territory level National Parks Associations, some of which also have a number of local sub-groups.

Sub-groups are also present in directed network campaigns, where the campaign has a core group which focuses on strategy and other centralized tasks. Information is then disseminated to local sub-groups, who have varying degrees of autonomy to plan their own local events while also participating in larger events led by the core team. This organizing structure is a common characteristic of successful campaigns, according to a review undertaken by NetChange consultancy (Mogus and Liacas 2016). Two examples of directed network campaigns in Australia are the Stop Adani campaign, with 126 local sub-groups working on the same campaign, and Extinction Rebellion, with 73 local sub-groups at the end of April 2020. Figure 8 presents models derived from our data that illustrate the conventional network of groups and campaigns in comparison to the structure of groups involved in directed network campaigns (see also Mogus and Liacas 2016).

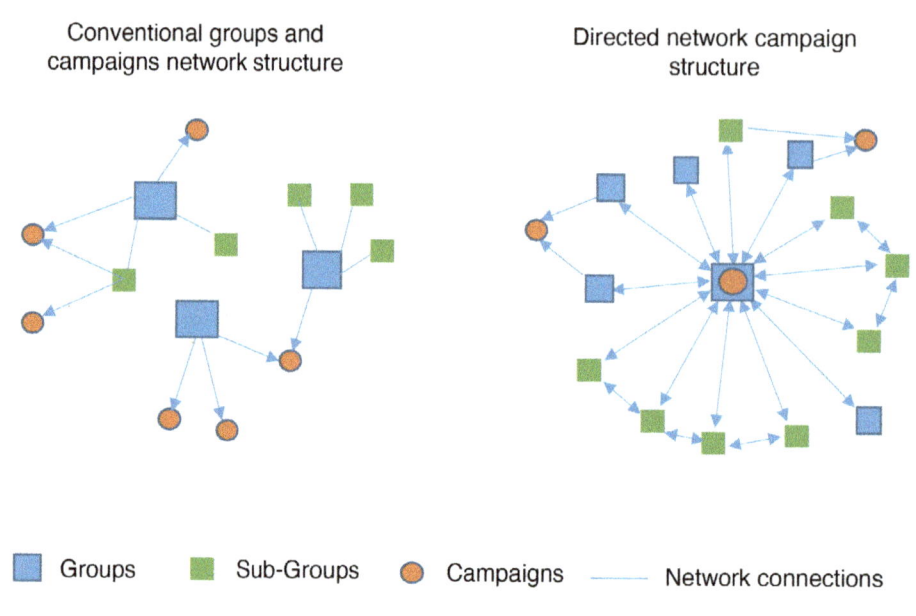

**FIGURE 8.** Comparison of Conventional and Directed Network Campaign Structures

As Figure 8 highlights, in both conventional and directed network structures, groups and sub-groups can engage in shared campaigns yet also operate independently. Each group and associated sub-group may also use their own communication channels, such as e-newsletters and social media pages. Therefore, to provide a comprehensive view of all events organized by groups across the movement (including civil resistance tactics), we searched all Facebook pages associated with the 492 environmental groups and their sub-groups. In

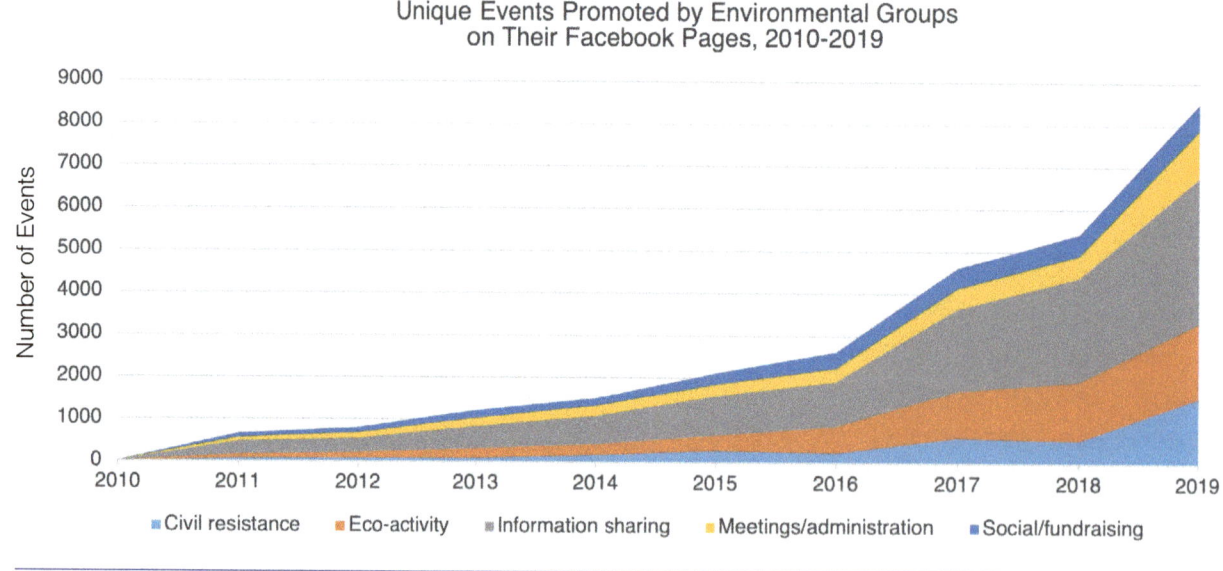

**FIGURE 9.** All Unique Events by Group Category, 2010–2019

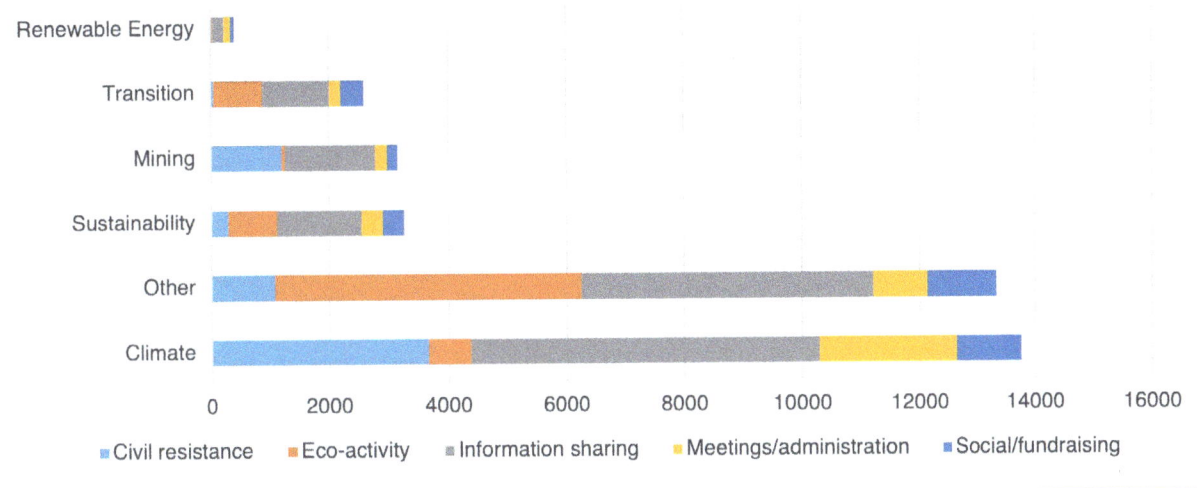

**FIGURE 10.** Types of Event Promoted by Environmental Groups

total, we identified 728 groups with Facebook pages, which together promoted 36,541 events between June 2010 and February 2020 (inclusive). Just under 9,000 of these events were cohosted, meaning events were duplicated across multiple Facebook groups. After removing duplicate events, 27,934 unique events remained. While we cannot confirm that all events took place, this large dataset provides a unique insight into the activities of environmental groups and groups more specifically engaged in civil resistance against climate change.

We grouped these events into the five categories listed in Table 3 (see **page 25**). Figure 9 presents the type and date of each event. As Figure 9 shows, our database indicates a substantial increase in events promoted by environmental groups in Australia between 2010 and 2019.

While the environmental movement as a whole uses a diverse range of tactics, the predominant activity is information sharing, followed by eco-activities. However, from 2018 to 2019 the number of unique civil resistance tactics promoted by groups rose substantially, increasing from 541 events in 2018 to 1,554 in 2019.

We then tried to determine which environmental issues are more likely to involve the use of civil resistance tactics. To do so, we separated each of the 728 groups into two categories. The first category includes groups focused on climate or the climate-related issues of mining, renewable energy, and sustainability. The second category includes groups focused on other environmental issues, such as conservation, nuclear waste or power, pollution, and waste. Figure 10 shows the different proportion of event types used by each.

In total, 6,330 events fit within our definition of civil resistance tactics (see Table 1 on **page 8**), of which 3,705 were unique (the remaining were cohosted by two or more groups). The majority of these civil resistance tactics were promoted by climate-focused groups and comprised 27% of all their events. Similarly, 38% of events organized by groups which focused on mining issues fit the definition of a civil resistance tactic. In contrast, groups focused on other issues such as conservation and waste organized 1,084 civil resistance tactics, which comprised only 8% of their total events. In total, 17% of all events across all groups involved some tactic of civil resistance.

**Civil Resistance Tactics**

What sort of civil resistance tactics are groups promoting? Figure 11 shows the type and proportion of civil resistance tactics promoted by the 728 groups in their Facebook channels.

As Table 7 indicates, groups focusing on climate change have promoted far more civil resistance tactics than groups working on other environmental issues, across all civil resistance categories. In this table the descriptions used by activist groups on their Facebook pages were used to categorize each tactic. For example, some groups described their social acts of omission as a "climate strike" while others described them as a "school strike." This is connected to the specific organizers of each event, with school-based and youth organizers most frequently describing the act as a "school strike," and other supporters naming them a "climate strike."

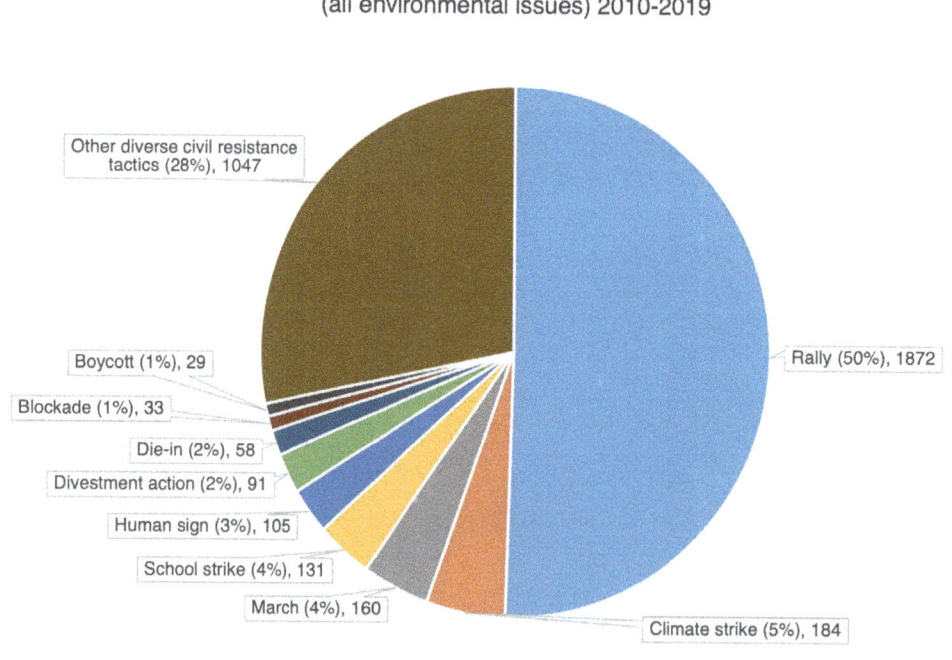

FIGURE 11. Most Common Civil Resistance Tactics, All Environmental Groups, 2010–2019

### Table 7. Unique Civil Resistance Tactics, Ordered by Category, 2010–2019

| CATEGORY | SUB-CATEGORY | MOST COMMON Civil Resistance Tactics (Most Common) | N | TOTAL NUMBER Climate Change-Related Groups | All Other Groups |
|---|---|---|---|---|---|
| Acts of Omission | Social | Climate strike | 184 (5%) | 349 (9%) | 19 (1%) |
| | | School strike | 131 (4%) | | |
| | | School walkout | 24 (1%) | | |
| | Economic | Divestment | 91 (2%) | 121 (3%) | 4 (0%) |
| | | Boycott | 29 (1%) | | |
| | | Strike | 1 (0%) | | |
| | Political | - | - | - | - |
| | Refraining | Canceled protest | 15 (0%) | 13 (0%) | 2 (0%) |
| Acts of Commission | Disruptive | Die-in | 58 (2%) | 243 (7%) | 13 (0%) |
| | | Blockade | 33 (1%) | | |
| | | Disruptive rally | 28 (1%) | | |
| | Creative | Assembly | 20 (1%) | 39 (1%) | 2 (0%) |
| | | Bicycle swarm/action | 15 (0%) | | |
| | | Read-in | 2 (0%) | | |
| Acts of Expression | | Rally | 1,872 (50%) | 2,280 (61%) | 624 (17%) |
| | | March | 160 (4%) | | |
| | | Human sign | 105 (3%) | | |
| Total | | | | 3,046 (82%) | 664 (18%) |
| | | | | 3,710 (100%) | |

The most common civil resistance tactic across all issues is the rally. In total, 1,872 unique rallies were promoted by groups between June 2010 and February 2020. The second most common civil resistance tactic was the climate strike (184 events). While the national climate strike was centrally organized by School Strike for Climate, many local events were held and promoted through groups' own unique Facebook events. The third most common civil resistance tactic was a march (160 events). Meanwhile, the most common target was a government (federal, state, or local; 438 rallies), followed by a member of parliament (422 rallies), and banks (169 rallies).

**Acts of Omission**

While only 10 percent of all civil resistance tactics were social acts of omission, most of these were climate and school strikes. This data highlights both the emergence of the use of strikes to drive action on climate change, as well as the strength of localized groups. The Australian School Strike for Climate organization operates as a directed network campaign, where a centralized group helped coordinate the nationwide strikes held in March and September

2019. The centralized group helped organize and promote the events while each sub-group promoted their own strikes in their local communities.

**Acts of Commission**

A wide variety of creative and disruptive acts of commission were also used (as shown in Table 7). The most common disruptive act of commission was the die-in (58 events), followed by blockades (33 events), a term that was generally used in two different ways: first, as a gathering that had an element of disruption attached to it (e.g., physically blocking MPs outside their office), and second, as a gathering at a blockade camp (e.g., the Adani coal mine camp, covered in more detail in Chapter 3). The third most common disruptive act of commission was disruptive rallies (28 events). In these events, supporters were invited to attend rallies and indicated that a disruptive element may occur. Finally, we note that the fourth most common disruptive act of commission were swarms (26 events), where groups of people stop traffic in busy urban areas for short periods of time. This tactic was used primarily by Extinction Rebellion.

The most common creative act of commission were assemblies, a social creative tactic we cover in more detail in the next section. Following this, bicycle swarms, where colorfully dressed participants biked through busy traffic areas, were promoted in 15 events, alongside two read-ins. Other creative civil resistance tactics used in the acts of commission category include street theatre, vigils, and mock funerals for the planet.

**Social Creative Interventions**

We are also interested in investigating the degree to which climate change groups are developing alternative climate solutions. These can include the creation of new parallel institutions or economic systems, a response which aligns with one of the three components found in the Great Turning model. In our analysis, when using data sourced from events promoted by groups on Facebook, we found that across the dataset there appears to be little evidence of these alternative responses occurring.

However, it may be that these creative interventions are occurring more frequently in slightly different forms. For example, although groups focused on renewable energy may not promote events linked to the creation of alternative economic systems, other evidence suggests they are seeking to work within the current system to enact meaningful change. Examples include the development of community-owned renewable energy systems and shared financial arrangements to fund solar panels at lower costs for the community.

In addition, groups such as Transition Towns aim to create more localized connections, using barter and sharing economies to support their goal. This is where data showing the substantial number of information sharing events such as workshops and public talks, as well as meetings, indicates that a vibrant information sharing economy is occurring within and between these groups.

Finally, Extinction Rebellion groups have created Citizen's Assemblies, where individuals consider and debate responses to various community challenges and democratically decide on strategies to address these challenges. The number of groups within the Australia Transition Town network (34) and the more than 30 renewable energy groups—as well as the emergence of networks such as the New Economy Network—indicates that this creative work is steadily increasing.

**Acts of Expression**

As noted, rallies were the most common civil resistance tactic. Using Beer's (2021) outline, we categorize this as an act of expression. The second most common act of expression was a march (160 events), followed by the human sign (105 events). In total 2,980 unique acts of expression were found across the dataset, including tactics as diverse as honkathons (12 events), twitter storms (5 events), and flash mobs (17 events).

**Organizational Status and Civil Resistance Tactics**

In this section, we present information identifying which groups use civil resistance tactics the most. Table 8 (on the following page) lists the ten groups that promoted the greatest number of civil resistance tactics, their number of sub-groups, and the year they were founded.

---

### Social Creative Interventions: The New Economy Network

The New Economy Network (NENA; **www.neweconomy.org.au**) aims to transform Australia's economic system. It is working to do this by fostering a network of individuals and groups undertaking innovative projects and initiatives that put ecological health and social justice first. The network has 10 regional hubs and 24 sectorial hubs focusing on issues such as:

- Ecological economics
- First Nation economics
- Post-extractivism
- Just transitions
- Cities and urban communities
- Women in the New Economy

In addition to the National Civil Society Strategy for a New Economy, the NENA annual conference, and New Economy Journal, the network supports more than 30 creative interventions including:

- Brisbane Tool Library
- MySequester community-based offsetting platform
- Galactic worker owned cooperative
- Food Connect Shed.

### Table 8. Number of Civil Resistance Tactics Promoted by Umbrella Groups

| GROUP | ORGANIZATIONAL STATUS | CIVIL RESISTANCE TACTICS | TOTAL EVENTS | NUMBER OF SUB-GROUPS (APRIL 2020) | FOUNDING YEAR |
|---|---|---|---|---|---|
| Extinction Rebellion | None | 1,256 | 3,895 | 77 | 2018 |
| Australian Youth Climate Coalition | Charity | 834 | 4,818 | 56 | 2006 |
| Stop Adani | None | 552 | 1,687 | 126 | 2016 |
| School Strike for Climate | None | 372 | 575 | 1 | 2018 |
| Knitting Nanas | None | 217 | 435 | 34 | 2012 |
| 350.org | Company | 169 | 496 | 8 | 2013 |
| Fossil Free | None | 159 | 996 | 22 | 2015 |
| Frack Free | None | 124 | 303 | 3 | 2013 |
| Galilee Blockade | None | 121 | 184 | 2 | 2017 |
| The Wilderness Society | Charity | 109 | 568 | 13 | 1976 |
| Total | | 3,913 | 13,957 | 342 | |

As Table 8 indicates, civil resistance tactics are used most by four groups: Extinction Rebellion, Australian Youth Climate Coalition, Stop Adani, and School Strike for Climate. These groups all have three characteristics in common. First, they are all focused on climate change. Second, they all share the primary characteristics of directed network campaigns. That is, each of them has a central core group focused on strategy that then disseminates plans outward to local sub-groups to implement via their local activities. This structure may enable more efficient use of resources, with the central core group able to frame the issue, coordinate activities, and gain access to allies and powerholders (Mogus and Liacas 2016). This then allows local groups to focus more exclusively on local mobilization.

The third notable characteristic of groups engaging in climate change civil resistance is that many sub-groups appear to have no legal status. In contrast to this, 58 percent of the total groups in the study population are registered organizations. This appears to indicate a disproportionate tendency of directed network campaigns with informal sub-groups to use civil resistance tactics and to engage in them more frequently than groups with formal organizational status and fewer or no sub-groups. This finding thus supports arguments suggesting that grassroots groups may be more open to including civil resistance in their campaign repertoire than professionalized groups (e.g., see Haddon and Jasny 2017). The freedom of grassroots groups to undertake activities without threat of losing their formal organizational status or funding may thus influence the tactics which groups choose to use. In addition, it also is apparent from this data that most of the groups actively engaging in disruptive civil resistance have emerged in the last five years.

**Outcomes of Climate Change Campaigns**

In the previous section we considered the characteristics of groups engaging in civil resistance on climate change and the types of tactics they are using. We now seek to consider the extent to which civil resistance is achieving its goals. However, there are significant challenges in linking specific civil resistance tactics to movement outcomes. First, movements involve multiple actors undertaking diverse activities in multiple arenas. Second, many activities organized by groups may be hidden from public view. In addition, methodologies used to assess the success or failure of particular actions are contested (e.g., Blackwood and Louis 2012; Hornsey et al. 2006). A final element of complexity concerns individual interpretations: activists' judgments of what constitutes a successful outcome can vary significantly depending on their own goals and expectations.

Many researchers have used different approaches to analyze the outcomes of conventional tactics in general, or civil resistance in particular. For example, some researchers use statistical analysis to ascertain whether social or environmental groups have an impact on the policy process (Burstein and Linton 2002). Other researchers have used content analysis of media coverage to compare the outcomes of violent versus nonviolent protest and provide substantial evidence that civil resistance movements advance democratization (Bartkowski

**FIGURE 12.** Climate Angels at Extinction Rebellion Declaration Day.

*Source: Wikimedia Commons. Photographer: Takver. Used under the Creative Commons Attribution-Share Alike 2.0 Generic license.*

2017). Each of these approaches yield valuable and informative insights, yet they are unable to identify whether specific tactics are directly linked to the achievement of specific goals.

Despite these challenges, it is possible to assess the outcomes of climate change resistance by identifying and tracking campaigns. Groups design campaigns as vehicles to promote messages and undertake activities specifically aimed at achieving campaign goals. Previous studies have demonstrated how studying these messages and activities can identify the characteristics more closely linked to successful campaign outcomes (Gulliver, Fielding, and Louis 2019). To further this work, we present information captured on 193 climate change campaigns identified on the website text of the 492 environmental groups in our study population, which was reviewed in 2017. For each campaign we identified the campaign name, target, and goal. We then conducted an online search in early 2020 for evidence regarding whether individual campaign goals had been successful, partially successful, or unsuccessful, or whether the outcomes remained unknown.

> **Brisbane Extinction Rebellion Die-in: May 26th, 2019**
>
> The "die-in" involves groups of activists engaging in a disruptive action symbolizing the effects of climate change in exacerbating mass extinctions. Staged around the world in 2018, the Brisbane event involved 250 activists laying down among the dinosaurs at the Queensland Museum. Media coverage focused on the range of activists participating, including families, workers, and retirees. This event signaled the power of the newly emerging Extinction Rebellion collective in Australia and its novel approach to civil resistance against climate change. The emergence of Extinction Rebellion also heralded new networks between existing groups, such as the Climate Guardians (as shown in Figure 12 on the previous page), and a merging of their distinctive and highly creative use of visuals to promote the climate change activism message.

A wide range of campaign targets were identified and grouped into five categories. The first of these categories encompasses political targets, such as a specific politician, a political position such as the federal environment minister, or a government entity such as the Queensland State Government. The second category is individuals, as with campaigns that ask individuals to change their behaviors, such as driving less and planting trees. The third category includes business targets, followed by community groups (category four) and health and education groups (category five). The final category includes campaigns where no explicit target was identified.

We classified successful campaigns as those where their goal was entirely achieved (for example, if new legislation was enacted as per the campaign demand). Unsuccessful outcomes were those where the goal had not been achieved (e.g., a coal mine development proceeded). Of course, unsuccessful campaigns may yet achieve their goals in the future, however our analysis recorded the outcome achieved by 2020. Partially successful outcomes were those where one part of the goal had been achieved, such as when one university announced a plan to divest from fossil fuels following a campaign to achieve university divestment. Finally, unknown outcomes occurred where evidence was not able to be gathered (such as with campaigns targeting individual behaviors).

Although this approach can yield valuable insights into connections between climate change campaigns and campaign outcomes, there are several limitations. First, most campaigns did not state when they were initiated, nor which specific events were associated with the campaign. As a result, our data is unable to identify which categories of civil resistance tactics were associated with greater or lesser degrees of success.

Similarly, while this approach enables an analysis of campaign goals and outcomes (as stated online by these campaigns), the extent to which the campaigns themselves influenced outcomes—as opposed to other external circumstances—remains unknown. Table 9 (on the following page) illustrates the number of climate change-related campaigns undertaken by groups in the study population and an assessment of their outcomes conducted in early 2020.

---

### A Just Transition

**Campaign name:** Fossil Free AGL
**Campaign group:** 350.org
**Campaign outcome:** Partially successful

In 2016–17, 350.org Australia ran the Fossil Free AGL campaign demanding that Australia's biggest polluter move out of the dirty energy business. At the time more than 80 percent of AGL's energy came from coal and they owned three of the eight biggest coal plants in the country. One of these is the Liddell power station near Sydney, which emits 13.70 million tons of greenhouse gases each year.

The campaign involved applying shareholder pressure on AGL, as well as a range of creative community actions organized by local Fossil Free AGL teams in Sydney, Melbourne, Brisbane, and Newcastle. The key campaign demand was to get AGL to outline a plan showing how it will transition out of all fossil fuel extraction, generation, and supply by 2026.

Sustained pressure had been applied by 350.org, as well as other groups including GetUp! In addition, reports had been completed demonstrating the Liddell power station's unreliability and inadequacy (Ogge 2018). In 2017, AGL announced they would be closing Liddell in 2022. In addition, they created the Liddell Innovation Project to address the energy, social, and economic impacts of a transition to a lower carbon future (Reid 2018). While AGL remains a major polluter, these announcements represent a partial campaign win for the climate movement.

### Table 9. Outcomes of Climate Change Campaigns, 2017–2020

| CAMPAIGN OUTCOME | TOTAL CAMPAIGNS N (%) | TARGET | | | | | |
|---|---|---|---|---|---|---|---|
| | | Political N (%) | Individual N (%) | Business N (%) | Unknown N (%) | Community Group N (%) | Health/ Education N (%) |
| Successful | 46 (24%) | 28 (28%) | 7 (17%) | 9 (31%) | 2 (11%) | - | - |
| Partially Successful | 34 (18%) | 19 (19%) | 4 (10%) | 9 (31%) | 1 (6%) | - | 1 (50%) |
| Unsuccessful | 49 (25%) | 35 (35%) | 3 (7%) | 2 (7%) | 8 (44%) | 1 (50%) | - |
| Unknown | 64 (33%) | 18 (18%) | 28 (67%) | 9 (31%) | 7 (39%) | 1 (50%) | 1 (50%) |
| Total | 193 | 100 | 42 | 29 | 18 | 2 | 2 |

As Table 9 highlights, 24% of the 193 campaigns had achieved successful outcomes, and 18% had achieved partial success. This means almost half of climate change campaigns organized in 2017 achieved some form of success (examples of campaign outcomes are listed in Table 10). Campaigns targeting businesses achieved the highest proportion of success (31%), closely followed by campaigns aimed at political targets (28%). More than half of all campaigns targeted political entities, including governments, politicians, and political candidates. The full list of all campaigns, outcomes, and links to evidence for the assessment of outcomes is available online at: **https://osf.io/f8pys/**.

### Table 10. Examples of Campaign Goals, Targets, and Outcomes

| GROUP | CAMPAIGN GOAL | CAMPAIGN TARGET | OUTCOME |
|---|---|---|---|
| Solar Citizens | Reject SA Power Network's application to charge unfair fees to solar owners | SA Power Networks (businesses) | Success |
| Quit Coal | Commit to the closure of Hazelwood, a coal power station in Victoria | Victorian State Government | Success |
| Stop CSG | Stop Santos CSG in the Pillaga | Santos (business) | Unsuccessful |
| The Transition Decade | Mobilize whole communities through a communication and partnership strategy, inform and activate citizens | Individuals | Unknown |

## Key Insights and Discussion

This chapter presents a wealth of data on the activities that environmental groups in Australia are engaged in. With over 700 groups promoting over 27,000 unique events, the movement is comprised of many groups undertaking a large number of activities. Our analysis of website text demonstrates that environmental groups focus on a range of issues and use a variety of tactics. Climate change emerges as an issue even in groups primarily focused on other challenges such as waste, conservation, and protection, and civil resistance tactics are used in conjunction with other conventional actions. Topic modeling indicates that the words most closely associated with climate change groups include "coal," "mine," "company," and "fossil." Thus, climate groups in Australia show a strong focus on contesting the continued extraction of fossil fuels, most specifically coal.

Our data also shows that new groups are rapidly emerging, especially those focused on climate change related issues and particularly over the last five years. The greatest number of new groups emerging over this period appear to be following a structure of directed network campaigns—that is, structured with a core team working on campaign planning with multiple autonomous sub-groups implementing campaign tactics. These groups—which include Stop Adani and Extinction Rebellion, and to a lesser extent the Australian Youth Climate Coalition—undertake the majority of civil resistance tactics, particularly acts of commission either through disruptive or creative intervention. This data therefore suggests that informal organizational structures composed of large numbers of local, grassroots groups, linked together in directed network campaigns, results in increased use of civil resistance tactics. While there are relatively few examples of civil resistance involving physical disruption (such as blockades and sit-ins), disruptive tactics appear to be used consistently by several groups and in increasing numbers.

Across the data used in this monograph we found very few incidents of violence on the part of civil resistance groups (neither violence against property nor persons), and no events used language conveying the use of violence connected with any tactics. This may reflect a consensus across these groups to reject violence and to maintain a high degree of nonviolent discipline as the most viable approach to achieve successful environmental outcomes. However, one relevant consideration is that groups may use veiled language and euphemisms in their promotional materials, which makes the categorization of such events and identification of the potential use of violence in the tactical repertoire difficult to ascertain.

We also considered the degree to which groups are engaging in social constructive interventions, particularly those highlighted by Sharp as nonviolent actions focusing on the creation of alternative social, economic, and governmental systems. Very few events explicitly promote these types of constructive interventions, although our data indicates that the number of these interventions are growing. The high number of Transition Town and Renewable Energy groups, the emergence of groups focusing on creating alternative social and economic structures such as the New Economy Network, and the high number of information sharing events indicate that substantial grassroots community effort is being directed into building more resilient and sustainable systems. Investigating the outcomes of these creative efforts systematically is a promising avenue for future research.

Finally, our analysis of the outcomes of climate change campaigns indicates that the climate change movement is achieving some degree of consistent success. While our data is limited in its ability to ascertain cause and effect, or to link specific civil resistance tactics to specific campaign outcomes, it is evident that many campaigns are achieving either full or partial success. Of the campaigns that stated targets, those directed toward business and political entities are achieving the most success. (This is not to say that campaigns working to change individual behaviors are not achieving success: many of these campaigns were coded as having "unknown" outcomes and may have achieved significant progress toward their ultimate aims.) This finding is important, as we know that showing that success is possible can help build greater support for a group's activities (Jugert et al. 2016; Klandermans 1997). It can also encourage more people to become involved in the group or cause (Bandura 2006; Fritsche, Barth, Jugert, Masson, and Reese 2017). Therefore, to help motivate supporters to become engaged, we suggest ensuring campaign targets and goals are achievable and clearly stated in communication materials created by climate change groups. Mechanisms for reporting against campaign goals and tracking goal achievement will serve to better monitor campaign progress. Furthermore, evaluating and conveying the successes that climate change groups have achieved may help increase the number of individuals engaging in grassroots environmental activism.

In this chapter we have presented data that provides a picture of the Australian environmental movement, as well as the civil resistance tactics used by groups focused on climate change. Much of the data we present here maps onto the movement frameworks identified in Chapter 2: the Great Turning, the Climate Insurgency, and the Political Process models. We discuss the findings from this mapping in detail in Chapter 5. In the next chapter we focus on two campaign case studies—the Stop Adani campaign and the Divestment campaign—in order to better understand how climate change groups are directing civil resistance tactics against business entities and what degrees of success they are experiencing.

# Chapter 3: Case Studies of Anti-Corporate Civil Resistance Campaigns

In Chapter 2, we briefly presented data on the outcomes of 193 climate change campaigns run by groups between 2017 and 2020, finding that campaigns targeting business entities were achieving the highest rates of success. While social movements do often target governments to generate policy or legislative change, detailed research has shown that a small number of corporations are linked to a significant proportion of greenhouse gas emissions. Almost two-thirds of total industrial carbon and methane emissions have been traced by Ekwurzel and colleagues (2017) to 90 carbon producers. There has been a long history of activism targeting corporate entities emerging primarily through the organized labor movement in the United States in the 1960s and 1970s. With the development of non-labor, anti-corporate campaigning focused on issues such as environmental and human rights transgressions, more than 200 such campaigns were waged even 25 years before the turn of the century (Manheim 2001), suggesting that businesses and corporations are now a major target for activists. One popular form of corporate campaigning is shareholder activism, where individuals use their rights as shareholders to bring about change within an organization. At least 839 globally listed companies were subjected to such activism in 2019 (Activist Insight 2020).

As discussed by Manheim (2001), anti-corporate campaigns attack the legitimacy of the corporation. This differs from traditional social movement activism which usually targets the government or government institutions. The effective workings of the state, in traditional analysis done by civil resisters, is based on the loyalty of the pillars of support (Popovic, Djinovic, Milivojevic, Merriman, and Marovic 2007), consisting, among others, of the police, military, bureaucracy, and business sector. Losing these pillars means leaders lose their ability to govern and exercise control, thus weakening the legitimacy of their claim to lead the state. Consequently, some argue that civil resistance is needed to undermine these pillars as a way to achieve movement goals (Ritter 2015). For corporate entities, the pillars can be different, based primarily around stakeholder relationships. These include customers, bankers, shareholders, and employees. The difference between these targets matter, as some scholars have shown how the type of target chosen can be highly influential in the type of tactic used. Walker and colleagues (2008) found in their review of protests between 1960 and 1990 in the United States that tactics such as rallies and lawsuits (the latter outside the traditional civil resistance repertoire) were more often used when targeting the state, while civil disobedience and other confrontational civil resistance tactics were more frequently used when targeting corporate and educational institutions.

Anti-corporate campaigns identify these relationships and seek out vulnerabilities in several areas. Manheim (2001) highlights five methods: defining and defending the moral high ground, bringing secondary financial pressure to bear on companies (e.g., through fund divestment), attacking shareholder value (where adverse publicity aims to reduce a company's share price), boycotting products and services, and using ligation or regulation. Different stakeholder groups can use different methods. For example, religious leaders can ask for more moral conduct, lawyers can take legal action against transgressions, and shareholders can express concern about effective management. In the environmental context there have been numerous examples of successful anti-corporate campaigning, such as Mattel and Nestlé's exposure as drivers of Indonesian deforestation through their supply chains, leading them to amend their supply chain policies (Lee 2011). Civil society action against corporations has also proven to be successful when targeting firms that are sensitive to reputation costs, where they operate in a political system with a robust rule of law and where the state is less dependent on their products (Chenoweth and Olsen 2016). However, resistance against corporations can also provoke countermeasures, such as when governments or employers pass anti-protest laws, weaken or marginalize unions, or victimize activists (Oxford Reference 2021). Some examples of this include Google's firing of employees protesting a range of Google policies (De Vynck, Bergen, and Gallagher 2019) or the intensified lobbying efforts in 2010 by the Australian mining industry to block legislation proposing a mining tax (Rennie 2016). Countermeasures can occur when campaigns target corporations that have the support of state powers in intelligence, security, and media, particularly those corporations involved in mining and resource extraction (Wilson Becerril 2018; see also Abrash Walton 2002).

Given the distinct opportunities and challenges around anti-corporate campaigns, and the particular role of corporations in driving the climate crisis, our dataset offers a rich opportunity to investigate civil resistance responses to corporate inaction on climate change. To do this we use a case study methodology to investigate two different anti-corporate campaigns that involve multiple groups over a long period of time and are well-known in the Australian context. The first, the Stop Adani campaign (**www.stopadani.com**), is a directed network campaign targeting one particular corporation proposing the development of a new thermal coal mine. The second is the Divestment campaign (**www.gofossilfree.org**), which seeks to persuade investors to sell out of fossil fuels entirely. This campaign is now a global effort with similarities to other directed network campaigns.

Both campaigns have multiple targets across corporate and state sectors. In addition, both have used conventional and civil resistance tactics and have been associated with a range of successes and failures. The choice of these two case studies allows consideration of the similarities and differences in targets, tactical choices, and campaign outcomes between campaigns that target a range of corporate entities. Thus, a closer analysis of these

**FIGURE 13.** Location of the Galilee Basin, Queensland

*Source: Wikimedia Commons. Created by user Galileebasin.
Creative Commons Attribution-Share Alike 4.0*

two campaigns enables us to better understand how climate change groups and their allies are targeting multinational corporations and associated entities, and to consider which tactics have been most effective in driving change. After presenting the case studies, we then discuss the insights that can inform future campaigns against corporations.

## Case Study 1: The Stop Adani Campaign

Stop Adani is a directed network campaign organized under the umbrella of the Stop Adani Alliance, with the help of a small team of paid organizers working for the Tipping Point (**www.tippingpoint.org.au**), an organization seeking to empower climate advocates to act effectively. The campaign, composed of 126 local, autonomous Stop Adani sub-groups of varying sizes (as of 2020), aims to halt the construction of a large thermal coal mine in northern Queensland. This coal mine, called the Carmichael project, is located in the undeveloped Galilee Basin in Central Queensland and, if constructed, will be the largest in Australia. The project was proposed by the Adani Group in 2010, a wholly owned subsidiary of India's Adani Group, which works primarily in port development and operations in India and has been linked to financial scandals and environmental offenses in India (Long 2017).

There are four primary reasons why significant public opposition to the project has emerged. First, the development of the mine will open up the Galilee Basin, with an additional eight proposed coal mines dependent on the development of rail and other infrastructure likely to be constructed once the Carmichael mine begins operation. Second, the coal projected to be extracted and subsequently combusted from these nine mines will release an estimated 705 million tons of carbon pollution into the atmosphere each year (Ritter 2018), which is similar to the annual emissions generated by countries such as Malaysia or Austria (Taylor 2015). Third, many associated effects related to the mine are anticipated to cause problems, such as the high volume of water required and the loss of Traditional Owners' native title rights to access the land covered by the mining tenements. Finally, the coal, destined for the Indian domestic market, is proposed to be shipped through the coal port terminal at Abbot Point near the Great Barrier Reef, a UNESCO World Heritage site, and it has been

**Timeline of Adani's Carmichael Mine**

**November 2010:** Adani begins approval process for two mines and a rail line

**May 2014:** Queensland Government gives preliminary approval subject to Federal Government approval

**July 2014:** Federal Government gives approval with 36 conditions (e.g., returning 730 ML water to the Great Artesian Basin every five years)

**August 2015:** Approval set aside by Federal Court due to vulnerable species assessments

**October 2015:** Re-approval granted by the Federal Government

**February 2016:** Final state approval granted

**April 2016:** Mining leases granted

**August 2016:** Indigenous challenge dismissed by the Federal Court

**December 2016:** Coal mine rail line and camp approved

**November 2017:** Project downsized from 60 to 10–15 million tons/year

**April 2018:** Groundwater plan receives federal government approval

**May 2019:** Black-throated finch conservation plan approved by Queensland Government after lengthy disputes, causing delays to project

**June 2019:** All final approvals granted, and construction begins

argued that shipping to support the mine and its exports will result in inevitable Reef degradation.

The Adani project has received support from both the Queensland State and the Australian Commonwealth Governments, resulting in initial approval being granted by the State Government in 2014, official approval in 2016, and all final outstanding plans and policies approved in 2019. Since its proposal in 2010, the project has generated substantial public discontent despite this political support, resulting in the emergence of one of the largest environmental campaigns in Australian history. Originally targeting Adani and its political backers, this campaign has simultaneously undertaken activism against the mining company, banks, insurance companies, contractors, and governments supporting the mine. This case study investigates the changing tactics used and the outcomes achieved by the campaign to date and considers how these have flowed into other civil resistance climate mobilizations across the country.

**Case Study Data and Analysis**

The Stop Adani campaign is a directed network campaign. As such, it is composed of many different groups working at a grassroots level in conjunction with a central group—the Stop Adani Alliance and Tipping Point—directing the campaign, all working toward the goal of stopping the mine (Mogus and Liacas 2016). To achieve this overarching goal, groups use different tactics and target different entities. In this analysis, we focus on tactics that target corporate entities.

Given the complexity of this directed network campaign and the multitude of groups and activities involved, data was acquired to address four areas: groups active within the campaign, the tactics they are using, their campaign targets, and the outcomes they are achieving. This data was acquired from three sources. We filtered our database of groups and actions to select only those active in the Stop Adani campaign. We also gathered information on the secondary targets and outcomes of the campaign from the Stop Adani and Market Forces websites.[7]

---

7 **http://www.marketforces.org.au**.

### Table 11. Groups Involved in the Stop Adani Campaign

| GROUP | NUMBER OF SUB-GROUPS | ORGANIZATIONAL TYPE | EVENTS FOCUSING ON ADANI CAMPAIGN | |
|---|---|---|---|---|
| | | | CIVIL RESISTANCE TACTICS | TOTAL NUMBER OF EVENTS |
| Stop Adani | 126 | No formal status | 552 | 1,687 |
| Australian Youth Climate Coalition | 12 | Charity | 311 | 497 |
| Galilee Blockade | - | No formal status | 121 | 184 |
| Extinction Rebellion | 10 | No formal status | 80 | 125 |
| 350.org | 7 | Company | 62 | 111 |
| Frontline Action on Coal | - | Inc. Association | 33 | 86 |
| Australian Conservation Foundation | 5 | Charity | 31 | 58 |
| Market Forces | - | Charity | 28 | 30 |
| Knitting Nanas | 8 | No formal status | 27 | 48 |
| Australian Religious Response to Climate Change | 5 | Charity | 25 | 44 |
| All other groups | 89 | Range | 283 | 531 |
| Total | 265 | | 1,315 | 3,232 |

**Groups Active in the Stop Adani Campaign**

The Stop Adani campaign consists of over 100 groups around the country composed of volunteers who work specifically on this campaign. A range of additional environmental groups also work on the campaign as part of their own activities. In order to identify the groups active on the campaign in our dataset, we searched the Stop Adani website to construct a list of local groups. We then searched through the Campaign Database (see Table 1 on **page 8** for a description) to identify other groups who note their involvement in the campaign on their websites. Finally, we searched through the Events Database—the collection of 36,541 events—to identify those associated with the Stop Adani campaign and the groups who organized them. Table 11 lists the groups who were involved in the campaign, their organizational type, and the number of Adani-related events they promoted on their Facebook pages.

In Table 11, we ordered groups according to the total number of events they promoted between 2010 and 2019. 3,232 events were related to the Stop Adani campaign, of which 1,315 (41%) were civil resistance tactics. The Stop Adani groups organized the largest proportion of events (41%), and a total of 265 groups organized an event related to the campaign.

**Tactics Used by Groups Active in the Stop Adani Campaign**

In this case study, we investigate the full range of events promoted by the groups, as well as the civil resistance tactics they used to target corporations. We used the Stop Adani Tactics dataset to group events into the same five categories presented earlier in Table 3 (see **page 25**): information sharing, eco-activities, meetings/administration, social/fundraising, and civil resistance tactics. Table 12 illustrates the number of events found in each category for each group, including cohosted events.

As shown in Table 12, Stop Adani groups organized 1,687 (52%) of the 3,401 events. The most common type of event was information sharing, followed by a civil resistance tactic. Of note was the prevalence of film screenings of the two documentaries created for the campaign, with 527 of the 1,511 information sharing events using this tactic. The spread of events across multiple groups indicates that the Stop Adani campaign is gaining support in a wide swathe of climate and environmental groups. Indeed, images from civil resistance tactics such as the large School Strike for Climate rally on September 20, 2019, demonstrates the way in which the campaign is being linked with the climate movement more broadly (Figure 14 on the following page).

### Table 12. Events Promoted by Groups Active in the Stop Adani Campaign

| GROUP | CIVIL RESISTANCE TACTICS | ECO-ACTIVITY | INFORMATION SHARING | MEETINGS/ ADMIN | SOCIAL/ FUNDRAISING | TOTAL |
|---|---|---|---|---|---|---|
| Stop Adani | 552 | 24 | 916 | 111 | 84 | 1,687 |
| Australian Youth Climate Coalition | 311 | 8 | 156 | 12 | 10 | 497 |
| Galilee Blockade | 121 | 2 | 50 | 3 | 8 | 184 |
| Extinction Rebellion | 80 | - | 41 | 1 | 3 | 125 |
| 350.org | 62 | 2 | 42 | 2 | 3 | 111 |
| Frontline Action on Coal | 33 | - | 50 | 2 | 1 | 86 |
| Australian Conservation Foundation | 31 | - | 26 | - | 1 | 58 |
| Climate Action Coffs Harbor | 19 | - | 27 | 1 | 6 | 53 |
| Knitting Nanas | 27 | - | 18 | 2 | 1 | 48 |
| Australian Religious Response to Climate Change | 25 | - | 16 | 2 | 1 | 44 |
| Total | 1,553 | 44 | 1,511 | 152 | 141 | 3,401* |

*Note: The total figures include all groups as well as the top 10 most active groups listed in the table.

We next consider the type of civil resistance tactics used in the Stop Adani campaign (see Table 13). Following Beer's (2021) categorization, we reviewed each of the 725 unique civil resistance tactics promoted by the involved groups and identified which category they fit best.

**FIGURE 14.** Stop Adani Logos at the School Strike for Climate Event.

*Source: Wikimedia Commons. Photographer: Julian Meehan.*
*Licensed under the Creative Commons Attribution 2.0 Generic license.*

### Table 13. Stop Adani Events Aligned with Categories of Civil Resistance

| CIVIL RESISTANCE CATEGORY | TYPE | ACTION | N | TOTAL |
|---|---|---|---|---|
| Acts of Omission | Economic | Boycott | 28 | 49 |
| | Social | School strike | 5 | |
| | Refraining | Protest canceled | 11 | |
| Acts of Commission | Disruptive | Blockade | 6 | 37 |
| | | Rally (with disruption) | 6 | |
| | Creative | Cycle action | 1 | 1 |
| Acts of Expression | | General rally | 520 | 738 |
| | | Human sign | 82 | |
| | | March | 26 | |
| Total | | | | 825 |

The most common type of civil resistance tactics used in the campaign were acts of expression. Most tactics in this category were rallies (520 events). This was followed by 82 events by Stop Adani groups around the country promoting a "human sign" to spell out the words "Stop Adani."

The second most common type of civil resistance tactics were acts of commission (i.e., doing something that the target does not want their opponents to do). Most of these were

---

### Camp Binbee: Stop Adani Blockade Camp

In 2019 a crowdfunding campaign was organized to enable a permanent frontline camp for the Adani blockade. Camp Binbee is located an hour west of Bowen, and a 14-hour drive north of Brisbane, the capital city of Queensland, the state in which the mine is located. Located by the banks of a river, Camp Binbee is equipped with a camp kitchen and various spaces for meetings and gatherings.

The camp is run by volunteers from Frontline Action on Coal, who invite activists to stay on site and engage in civil resistance to stop the mine. These actions take place across significant distances, with the Adani head office located in Townsville (a 3 hours' drive north) and the mine site spread across a vast area ranging from 3 to 8 hours' drive west of the camp.

Since the camp was first set up, hundreds of nonviolent creative and disruptive actions have occurred. Activists have chained themselves to the existing coal rail line, the Abbott Point coal terminal has been blockaded, and countless interventions against sub-contractors have helped delay work on the site. In addition, the camp has served as a meeting point for groups to visit, including medical professionals, artists, and faith groups. With the mine projected to take years to construct, Camp Binbee will persist.

disruptive actions involving some sort of disruptive protest. The most common was a rally involving a component of disruption (six unique events). Examples of these include a protest outside a corporate or government office wherein a small group of activists also enter the building and refuse to leave. An equally common disruptive action was an event specifically listed as an occupation, particularly an occupation of businesses engaged in work for the Adani coal mine. Across the Stop Adani dataset we found only one example of creative acts of commission—in this case, a cycle action.

The most common act of omission was the boycott. This tactic was only used over a short period of time during a Stop Adani "Week of Action." Local groups were encouraged to boycott a particular company—Tradelink—that was offering supplies to the Adani coal mine. Groups affiliated with Galilee Blockade, Extinction Rebellion, Frontline Action on Coal, and Stop Adani all participated in the boycott. In total, 11 "refraining" events were identified in the dataset. Five of these events referred to protests against the banks that were canceled after the banks committed to not fund the Adani coal mine project. Another four events were canceled after AECOM engineering consultancy committed to halt work for Adani. The remaining three canceled events were planned bus trips up to Camp Binbee to blockade the coal mine.

### Primary and Secondary Targets

Campaigns target holders of power (Tilly 1999), including political entities, corporations, and individuals. It is helpful to also distinguish between primary and secondary targets, particularly when considering sustained campaigns directed toward large multinational companies like Adani. The primary target is the entity that is able to meet activists' demands, which in this case study is the Adani corporation itself. Secondary targets constitute the primary target's pillars of support, such as banks, other businesses, and politicians. These secondary targets may be more accessible to activist agitation than the primary target itself (Bobo, et al. 2001). In addition, secondary targets may hold power over the primary target. For example, banks hold significant power over corporations through their ability to fund projects. In this case study we investigate the extent to which the

**FIGURE 15.** Human Sign Action

On October 7, 2017, 40 groups around the country organized a photoshoot for a human sign spelling out "Stop Adani." Thousands of supporters joined the event, resulting in images which would be used by the campaign to share its message across newspapers, social media and videos. (Image credit: Stop Adani Melbourne, License CC By 2.0)

campaign against Adani (the primary target) also involves actions directed toward secondary targets.

An effective tool for visualizing the relationships and entities who benefit from the status quo is called tactical mapping. This involves sketching out targets for intervention and mapping potential tactics that would have the greatest influence on those targets (Johnson and Pearson 2009). Although our data does not reveal whether tactical mapping was undertaken in the Stop Adani campaign, we identified a range of targets in different relationships with the Adani company. In order to identify these targets, we reviewed the text in each event promoted on Facebook across our group database. We also tracked the change in targets over time. While many Facebook events did not specifically state a target for their civil resistance tactics (see Table 14), the most commonly named secondary targets were political entities, business and banks.

### Table 14. Most Common Targets Identified in Facebook Event Text

| | CIVIL RESISTANCE TARGETS | NUMBER OF EVENTS |
|---|---|---|
| **Primary target** | Adani | 37 |
| **Secondary targets** | Federal Member of Parliament | 147 |
| | GHD (engineering company) | 94 |
| | Tradelink (plumbing retail company) | 50 |
| | Commonwealth Bank | 37 |
| | Queensland Government | 30 |
| | Prime Minister | 29 |
| | Federal Government | 26 |
| | AECOM (engineering company) | 20 |
| | State and Federal Governments | 14 |
| | Westpac Bank | 9 |
| **Target unstated** | | 262 |
| **Total** | | 755 |

We also tracked the change in secondary targets over time. As demonstrated in Figure 16 (on the following page), while the primary target has remained the Adani Corporation throughout the campaign, secondary targets have changed substantially. The targets have changed according to the issues of the day and also the degree to which targets agreed to the campaign goals. Before August 2017, banks were predominantly targeted, when a major focus of the campaign was to demand that the "big four" Australian banks commit to not funding the coal mine. The central core group designed nationwide "Days of Action" targeting these banks, resulting in all four banks publicly announcing their intention to not fund the mine. Chinese and Korean Banks pledged similar commitments as well.

In early 2019, media reports identified contractors and engineering consultancy businesses—such as GHD and AECOM—who were allegedly negotiating with Adani to secure contracts to build the mine and associated infrastructure. As a result, the secondary targets shifted to these contracting businesses. When these secondary targets capitulated to the campaign goals, the campaign targets shifted again to a small number of infrastructure providers (namely, rail companies).

**Outcomes of Civil Resistance Tactics Against Secondary Targets**

We now consider the link between successful outcomes and the number of civil resistance tactics or type of secondary target. To identify which secondary target has agreed to the campaign demands, we collected data compiled by Market Forces.[8] This Australian not-for-profit organization regularly updates successful outcomes against secondary targets on their webpage and groups them into the categories used in Table 15. An outcome is defined as "won" if the target agrees to not associate in any way with the Adani coal mine or to cut already established ties (see column 3 in Table 15, which highlights the number of successful outcomes).

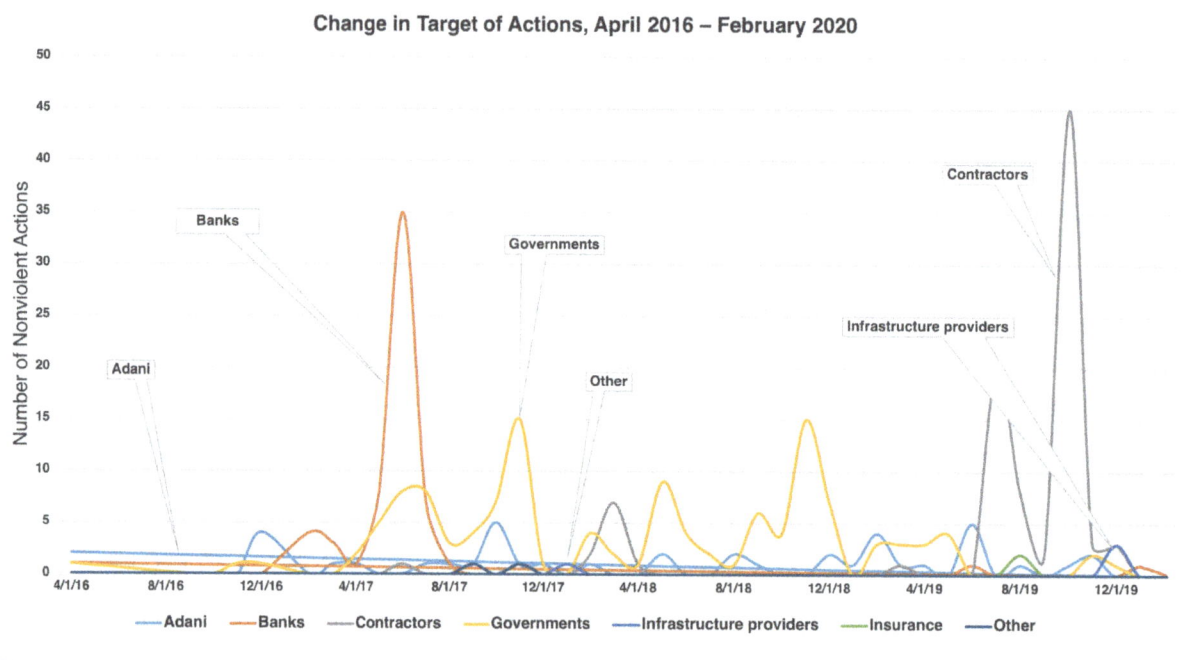

FIGURE 16. Change in Stop Adani Targets over Time

---

8   www.marketforces.org.au.

### Table 15: Number of Secondary Targets by Sector

| COMPANY SECTOR | NUMBER OF COMPANIES | | NUMBER OF CIVIL RESISTANCE ACTIONS |
| --- | --- | --- | --- |
| | TARGETED | WON (%) | |
| Finance | 60 (41%) | 46 (77%) | 62 |
| Construction and engineering | 48 (33%) | 12 (25%) | 96 |
| Insurance | 34 (23%) | 4 (12%) | |
| Coal haulage | 3 (2%) | 1 (33%) | 4 |
| Total | 145 | 63 (43%) | 160 |

As Table 15 illustrates, groups secured 63 wins against secondary targets, with the most wins involving targets that were going to finance the mine. In this context, a win means that the target made a public announcement to not become involved with the Adani mine. Beyond banks, several construction and engineering firms have also ruled out working on the mine. The campaigns against insurance companies achieved a 10% success rate, and one of the three coal haulage companies was successfully targeted (33% success rate). This data suggests that directing actions at secondary targets to remove corporate pillars of support may be highly effective, at the very least, in delaying the development of large projects. In addition, our data suggests that short-term, high-intensity activism against certain secondary targets may be more likely to result in success. At the same time, it must be acknowledged that despite these wins, Adani company often has managed to ultimately find a provider of services. Furthermore, some companies have reneged on their pledge and continue to work with Adani despite commitments made otherwise. Despite these limitations, the success in securing commitments from banks and contractors highlights the power of this campaign to make the development of the mine much more difficult for the Adani Corporation. In addition to corporate secondary targets, the Stop Adani campaign has undertaken civil resistance against federal, state, and local levels of government. For example, activists targeted NAIF, a federal government funding body, resulting in the commitment of the Queensland State Government to veto taxpayer funding for mining infrastructure. The Stop Adani campaign has listed a series of wins against government secondary targets on their website,[9] a selection of which are included in Table 16 (on the following page). However, while the campaign has achieved some significant wins against government secondary targets, the mine now progresses with full government approval.

---

9   http://www.stopadani.com/stopadani_successes.

### Table 16. Selection of Wins Against Government Secondary Targets

| DATE | SUCCESSFUL OUTCOME | TARGET |
|---|---|---|
| 12/12/2017 | Premier of Queensland makes vetoing $1b loan to Adani's coal project the first official act of her reelected government. | Queensland State Government |
| 6/06/2018 | Townsville Council re-directs $18.5m of ratepayers' funds away from Adani airport. | Townsville Council |
| 9/06/2018 | The Queensland Government announces that it will uphold Queensland's environmental laws and prosecute Adani for a coal spill into sensitive wetlands at a site they are developing. | Queensland State Government |
| 5/03/2019 | The Queensland Government rejects Adani's Black Throated Finch Management Plan and added extra conditions that needed to be satisfied. | Queensland State Government |
| 6/12/2019 | The Australian Conservation Foundation wins their legal challenge to Adani's water scheme approval as the Federal Government concedes the case. | Federal Government |
| 7/16/2019 | The Queensland Government announced it will prosecute Adani for providing "false and misleading" information in its Annual Report to Government. | Queensland State Government |

### Siemens International AGM Protest

The Stop Adani campaign gained international attention when it targeted the Siemens corporation, asking the CEO to cancel a contract with Adani to provide rail signaling services. A series of high-profile tactics resulted in international support for the campaign. Over 330,000 people signed a German petition sent to Siemens, a Sydney school striker delivered a letter to the CEO, and a Stop Adani delegation travelled to Germany to attend the Siemens shareholders' Annual General Meeting (AGM). Although many thousands of supporters contacted the company, yet Siemens decided to continue their work with Adani. Although the campaign did not achieve the outcome it desired, Siemens remains vulnerable to direct action once on-site work begins.

### Case Study 2: The Divestment Campaign

In this section we consider the characteristics and outcomes of the Divestment campaign. Divestment refers to the goal of calling on organizations to sell off or otherwise reduce holdings in companies associated with fossil fuels. It also asks organizations to immediately freeze new investments in fossil fuel companies and end fossil fuel sponsorship.

The demand for organizations to divest as a means of driving meaningful action on climate change has been around since the early 1990s (Ayling and Gunningham 2017), when Greenpeace was using this approach to convince insurance companies to de-invest in fossil fuels (Leggett 1993). More recent incarnations were promoted in 2012 with Bill McKibben's publication of "Global Warming's Terrifying New Math" in *Rolling Stone* magazine (McKibben 2012). Before this, similar activism had occurred during the United States 2007 presidential primary campaigns (Ayling and Gunningham 2017). In 2008, 350.org was established, with their organizational name referring to what is considered a safe limit for atmospheric $CO_2$ levels, beyond which dangerous climate change is risked (Hansen, et al. 2008). With the publication of McKibben's *Rolling Stone* article, the campaign grew and was able to target the 200 leading publicly traded fossil fuel companies. The campaign went global, with new organizations developing in Australia and partners and allies of 350.org identified in 187 other countries (Ayling and Gunningham 2017).

The primary goal of the Divestment campaign is to achieve a complete break with fossil fuels (Ayling and Gunningham 2017). For this purpose, the campaign also aims to raise awareness of climate change and the role of corporations within it. A secondary goal is to bring the stability and reliability of the fossil fuel industry and its profits into doubt through highlighting the risk of stranded assets—those assets which lose value and are unable to be recovered by investors (Fischer and Baron 2015). The campaign focuses on investors, primarily and initially universities. In more recent years, the campaign has targeted organizations such as local, state, and federal governments, banks and other financial institutions, pension funds, and religious organizations.

The campaign has been successful both internationally and in Australia. For example, at the time of this writing, over 1,300 organizations around the world have publicly committed to divestment by early 2021, including large groups such as the World Council for Churches and the Norwegian Sovereign Wealth Fund. However, whether this success continues or translates into actual emissions reduction is less clear. Some authors argue that it is unlikely the campaign will cause any direct effect on the valuations of fossil fuel companies, although they may impact coal stock prices (Ansar, Caldecott, and Tilbury 2013). A combination of state ownership, loss of shareholder engagement, and the quick and easy buy up of divested stocks by other investors means that their asset prices are to some extent protected. Goals such as a loss of social license to operate—that is, promoting a message that investing in fossil fuels is morally wrong—is what may drive divestment activists at present and can indirectly lead to change in market norms and the stigmatization of the fossil fuel industry (Ansar, Caldecott, and Tilbury 2013). However, there has also been pushback from various organizations around the world, such as the Minerals Council of Australia, which has accused divestment activists as acting illegally (Saunders 2014). In addition, some industry advocates have sought to make secondary boycotts—campaigns designed to prevent the supply of goods and services—illegal, with no success to date (Seccombe 2019).

In this case study we investigate the groups involved in the Divestment campaign in Australia to ascertain the degree to which civil resistance tactics have been used by the campaign and what outcomes have been achieved.

**Case Study Data and Analysis**

Like the Stop Adani campaign, the Divestment campaign is a directed network campaign. It is composed of many different groups working at a grassroots level all working to drive divestment commitments from their primary target (Mogus and Liacas 2016). However, the Divestment campaign differs from Stop Adani in that there is a very large number of primary targets. Whereas the Stop Adani campaign has only the one (the Adani mine), the Divestment campaign is comprised of a range of activist groups focused on distinct primary targets in different sectors such as healthcare and education. As noted above, although the Divestment campaign operates globally, we focus exclusively on the Australian groups active in the campaign and the outcomes of the campaign against Australian targets.

Compared to the Stop Adani campaign, it is more difficult to measure success in the Divestment campaign, primarily because divestment is a multi-staged process. A public statement by an organization expressing a commitment to divest is merely the first step in achieving actual financial divestment. In this case study we count public divestment commitments from organizations in Australia as a successful campaign outcome, while noting that the actual process of divesting may or may not occur. Whether organizations follow through with divestment commitments depends on several internal organizational factors, such as leaders' motivations and experiences as well as changes in the investment environment (Abrash Walton 2018a). As such, longitudinal research following up links between divestment commitments and divestment actions would be of great value for better understanding longer term outcomes of the Divestment campaign.

Data on the campaign was gathered from three primary sources. Our database of groups and actions was filtered to select only those active in the Divestment campaign, and information on the outcomes of Divestment campaigns was compiled from the Divest Australia and 350.org webpages. The following four sections detail results from this data.

**Groups Active in the Divestment Campaign**

The Divestment campaign was initiated in Australia by 350.org in 2013, and it quickly grew to a point where the organization could employ staff. They soon helped develop local 350.org groups, supported the formation of university campus-based Fossil Free groups, and shared campaign information with other environmental groups around the country.

Information on these groups was compiled into a database dedicated to the Divestment campaign. A total of 29 Fossil Free Australia and 350.org groups were identified, along with 27 other groups who promoted Divestment campaigns or divestment related events (see Table 17). Unlike the Stop Adani campaign, where a large range of groups organized many events, the Divestment campaign appears to be primarily dependent on just two groups: Fossil Free and 350.org.

Table 17. The Divestment Campaign: Groups, Sub-Groups, Their Status, Civil Resistance Tactics Used, and Number of Events Associated with Each

| UMBRELLA GROUP | ORGANIZATIONAL STATUS | NUMBER OF SUB-GROUPS INVOLVED | CIVIL RESISTANCE TACTICS | TOTAL EVENTS |
|---|---|---|---|---|
| 350.org | Company | 8 | 155 | 462 |
| Fossil Free | Charity | 21 | 130 | 882 |
| Australian Youth Climate Coalition | Charity | 4 | 36 | 36 |
| Extinction Rebellion | No formal status | 7 | 10 | 10 |
| Healthy Futures | Company | - | 2 | 2 |
| Market Forces | Charity | - | 2 | 2 |
| TUU Enviro Collective | No formal status | - | 2 | 2 |
| Uni Students for Climate Justice | No formal status | - | 2 | 2 |
| Bendigo Sustainability Group | No formal status | - | 2 | 2 |
| Other environmental groups | Range | 9 | 9 | 9 |
| Total | | 54 | 409 | 1,573 |

As with the Stop Adani campaign, events were dominated by the two main umbrella groups, especially Fossil Free, who also dominated in terms of both the number of events promoted on their Facebook pages and the number of civil resistance tactics used within the campaign. Of the more than 1,000 divestment-related events promoted on Facebook pages, 85 percent of these were undertaken by these two umbrella groups.

This suggests a significant difference between the Stop Adani and Divestment campaigns regarding whether other groups within the wider Australian environmental movement are engaged in their campaigns. For example, the data indicates that the Divestment campaign involved 54 groups and promoted 1,573 events, while Stop Adani involved 265 groups and promoted 3,232 events. Out of the 74 Extinction Rebellion groups identified in our overall database, only ten promoted an event specifically focused on the Divestment campaign. Similarly, only four groups that were focused on environmental issues outside of climate change organized divestment-related events. It thus appears that while the Divestment campaign has been sustained for a longer period than the Stop Adani campaign, it has involved fewer groups and promoted fewer events.

**Tactics Used in the Divestment Campaign**

We used the Divestment Tactics dataset to group events into the same five categories as those used for the Adani tactics: information sharing, eco-activities, meetings/administration, social/fundraising, and civil resistance tactics. As shown in Table 18, divestment events promoted on Facebook pages are spread across all event categories, with the most common event types being information sharing and civil resistance tactics.

### Table 18. Range of Events Promoted in Divestment Campaign (Including Cohosted Events)

| UMBRELLA GROUP | CIVIL RESISTANCE TACTICS | ECO-ACTIVITY | INFORMATION SHARING | MEETINGS/ ADMIN | SOCIAL/ FUNDRAISING | TOTAL |
|---|---|---|---|---|---|---|
| Fossil Free | 159 | 68 | 362 | 284 | 123 | 996 |
| 350.org | 169 | 19 | 257 | 26 | 25 | 496 |
| Australian Youth Climate Coalition | 36 | - | - | - | - | 36 |
| Extinction Rebellion | 17 | - | - | - | - | 17 |
| Bendigo Sustainability Group | 8 | - | - | - | - | 8 |
| Healthy Futures | 2 | - | - | - | - | 2 |
| Market Forces | 2 | - | - | - | - | 2 |
| TUU Enviro Collective | 2 | - | - | - | - | 2 |
| Uni Students for Climate Justice | 2 | - | - | - | - | 2 |
| Blue Mountains Climate Action | 2 | - | - | - | - | 2 |
| Climate Action Canberra | 1 | - | - | - | - | 1 |
| All other groups | 1 | - | - | - | - | 1 |
| Total | 409 | 87 | 619 | 310 | 148 | 1,573 |

The number of events promoted by groups active in the campaign in our dataset is heavily skewed toward Fossil Free and 350.org sub-groups. In keeping with the pattern observed across the wider environmental movement (see Chapter 2), the highest number of events are related to information sharing. These include organizing market stalls, public forums, and film nights. Understandably, there are relatively few eco-activities organized by groups involved in the campaign, and there are a similar number of administrative events and civil resistance tactics.

Of the 409 civil resistance tactics identified in Table 18, 350 of these were unique (i.e., not cohosted between two or more groups). Table 19 highlights the most common types of civil resistance promoted by groups active in the campaign.

### Table 19. Types of Civil Resistance Used in the Divestment Campaign

| CIVIL RESISTANCE CATEGORY | TYPE | ACTION | N | TOTAL |
|---|---|---|---|---|
| Acts of Omission | Economic | Divestment day | 71 | 113 |
| | | Bank divestment | 23 | |
| | Social | Climate strike | 6 | |
| | | School strike | 5 | |
| | Refraining | | 3 | |
| Acts of Commission | Disruptive | Rally (with disruption) | 5 | 16 |
| | | Blockade | 4 | |
| | | Die-in | 12 | |
| | Creative | Assembly | 1 | 1 |
| Act of Expression | | General rally | 138 | 218 |
| | | March | 15 | |
| | | Human sign | 12 | |
| Total | | | | 348 |

The most common category of civil resistance tactics was an act of expression, with 218 actions. Of these, 138 were various types of rallies with no identifiable disruptive element. The second most popular activity were divestment days (from the acts of omission category), where individuals are encouraged to divest their own finances from institutions supporting the fossil fuel industry. This suggests that the Divestment campaign targets organizations and individuals, unlike the Stop Adani campaign where the primary and secondary targets are organizational entities associated directly with the mine. Finally, some groups involved in the campaign also promoted events related to the school strike, die-ins, and human sign activities, suggesting that these groups are more likely to promote multiple campaigns in addition to Divestment.

**Targets and Outcomes**

Across our dataset of groups and actions between 2010 and 2019, we identified 36 targets specifically mentioned by groups undertaking divestment actions. We also constructed a dataset of divestment announcements by Australian organizations from 2015 to 2019. These announcements are listed on the 350.org Australia website and the Divest Australia website.

## Table 20. Australian Divestment Targets and Announcements by Organization Type, 2015–2019

| TYPE OF ORGANIZATION | TARGETED | ANNOUNCEMENTS BY COMPANIES TO DIVEST |
|---|---|---|
| Superannuation funds | 1 | 118 |
| Local councils/governments | 9 | 45 |
| Faith-based organizations | - | 28 |
| Philanthropic foundations | - | 19 |
| Educational institutions | 20 | 10 |
| NGOs | - | 5 |
| For-profit corporations | 4 | 4 |
| Healthcare institutions | - | 4 |
| Financial institutions | 2 | 1 |
| Mining companies | - | 1 |
| Total | 36 | 235 |

As Table 20 demonstrates, despite activist groups in the Divestment campaign only targeting 36 specific entities, many other organizations have chosen to divest over the same time period. The majority of divestment announcements were made by superannuation funds (pension funds) and local councils. Superannuation funds hold significant funds and thus represent important corporate wins for the Divestment campaign. However, aside from these funds very few of these announcements have been made by companies; only six of the 235 announcements were made by corporations, mining companies, or financial institutions. Furthermore, despite the large number of Fossil Free groups exclusively focused on encouraging universities to divest, only ten (out of 43 total universities in Australia) have made public announcements regarding their intentions to divest.

The number of divestment announcements occurring independently of any observable activism suggests other factors are influencing organizations' choices to divest. In particular, very large numbers of superannuation funds and many government entities are divesting without specific activist pressure. On the other hand, only half of the educational institutions targeted have made divestment announcements. This implies that campaign activities may not be directly linked to the occurrence of divestment announcements (see also Abrash Walton 2018b). Given the financial significance of divestment announcements, there may be many other factors influencing an organization's choice to divest. Some organizations may refuse to divest despite sustained activist pressure, and others may divest independently or prior to any activist pressure.

Furthermore, while the number of divestment announcements made by companies between 2015 and 2019 is impressive, the number of announcements appears to be declining since their peak in mid-2015. In Figure 17, a "win" means the organization made an

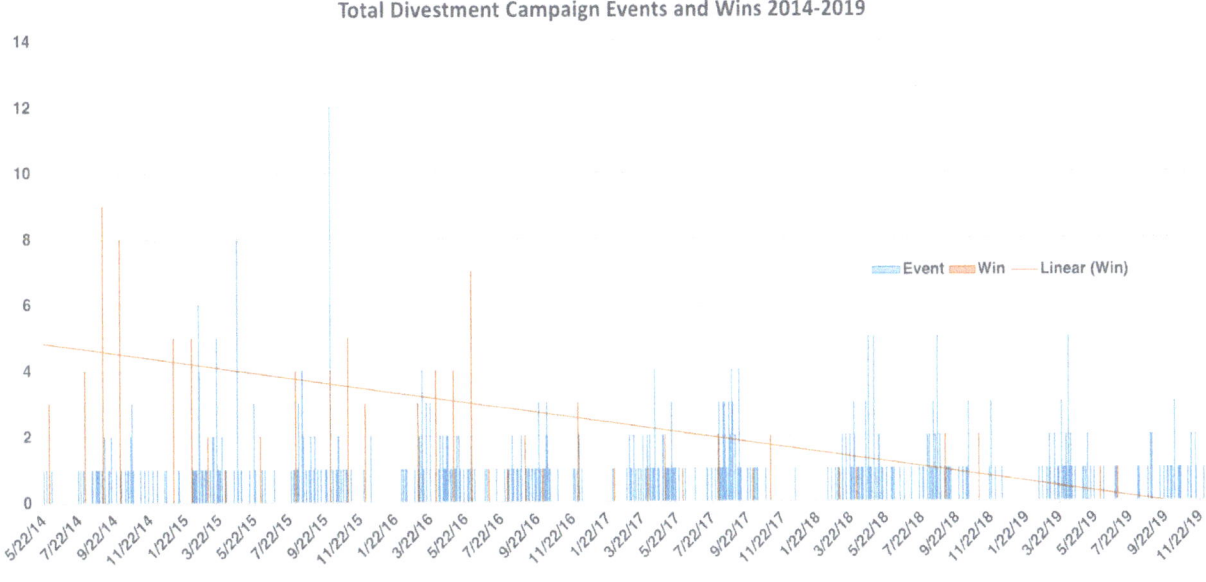

FIGURE 17. Divestment Campaign Events and Divestment Announcements, 2014–2019

announcement to divest from fossil fuels, and events refer to the tactics used by the campaign over this period.

There are a few possible explanations for why this decline may have occurred. First, the high number of announcements in the early years may be linked to lower hanging fruit. Organizations predisposed to divestment may have made early announcements, whereas in later years driving divestment commitments may require more sustained pressure by the campaign, with sophisticated tactical innovation and escalation. Given that the number of events promoted by groups since 2014 has declined, this suggests that activist groups may have been unable to sustain the high pressure required. This may be particularly difficult for groups targeting educational institutions, where many activists are transient students with other significant demands on their time.

Another potential reason for the reduction in successful announcements relates to challenges experienced by 350.org, the primary organization driving this directed network campaign. This organization directly supports 33 of the 79 groups active on the Divestment campaign and has endured a prolonged government inquiry into its charitable status after organizing the Breakfree Blockade. This highly visible event in May 2016 involved 2,000 people blockading Newcastle Coal Port, the world's largest coal port. 350.org's role in this event sparked a long-running investigation by Australia's Charities and Not-for-profits Commission into whether the organization was "promoting unlawful activity" (Kirkwood 2017). Although 350.org ultimately maintained its charitable status, the investigation diverted considerable resources from them (Coorey 2017). The impact of these issues is important, as the 33 groups supported by 350.org together undertook 533 (88%) of the 604 events.

Finally, we conjecture that the rise of other climate change groups and climate change activism strategies—such as the use of disruptive civil resistance tactics by Climate Emergency Declarations and Extinction Rebellion—may have co-opted some of the energy of the Divestment campaign in Australia. Although our data is unable to delve into this possibility, future research could investigate in detail how these dynamics may interact.

## Case Study Insights and Discussion

In this chapter we undertook an investigation into two campaigns targeting corporate entities. The first of these was the Stop Adani campaign, which aims to stop the multinational Adani Corporation from building a new thermal coal mine in northern Queensland. The second was the Divestment campaign, which targets a range of institutions asking them to divest any financial assets linked in fossil fuels. We analyzed each of the case studies in terms of:

- the number and types of groups that comprise the campaigns
- the conventional versus civil resistance tactics used
- how the civil resistance tactics map onto Beer's typology
- the targets of the tactics
- the successes achieved by each of the campaigns

In terms of the Stop Adani campaign, our data shows that this campaign has directed its efforts toward a wide range of secondary targets, including potential contractors for the mine construction, banks, insurance entities, and local, state, and federal governments. The longitudinal data shows that while the campaign has not yet achieved the goal of stopping the coal mine, substantial successes have accrued through persistent civil resistance tactics directed at the full range of secondary targets. In particular, the use of disruptive acts of omission by a small number of groups against specific targets—such as blockades and sit-ins in corporate offices and contractors' workplaces—has achieved considerable success. Through securing commitments by banks and potential contractors not to work on the mine, activists have delayed construction on the Adani project by nine years.

The second case study looked at the Divestment campaign. This campaign targets a wide range of corporate and government entities, including universities, banks, and local council and community organizations. The data shows that activists have secured divestment commitments from numerous Australian organizations, although the extent to which these

> ### La Trobe University Divestment Commitment
>
> In May 2016, La Trobe University in Melbourne became the first university in Australia to commit to a complete divestment from fossil fuels within five years. The commitment followed campaigning by staff and students on campus through 350.org, which provided support from a dedicated national campus divestment coordinator, as well as resources and guides to help plan the campaign.
>
> While La Trobe University was the first to commit to full divestment, Australian National University (ANU) led the way in 2014 by divesting from seven resource companies and selling $16m worth of shares, after 82% of students voted in favor of ANU divesting. This commitment was obtained after three years of student campaigning by the ANU Environment Collective, and was followed by a wave of media and political criticism. Despite ongoing campaigning, including the submission of an open letter signed by 450 academic and general staff, ANU still has holdings in fossil fuel companies. In total, 9 of the 43 Australian universities have committed to fully or partially divesting from fossil fuel supported companies.

translate into actual divestment is unknown. It is also unclear whether successful divestment commitments have any measurable effect on fossil fuel companies if there are an equivalent number of new buyers willing to buy those divested shares. As with the Stop Adani campaign, a range of civil resistance and other tactics have been used by activist groups against their targets. However, unlike the Stop Adani campaign, disruptive civil resistance does not appear to be linked to successful outcomes.

As such, these case studies indicate both the opportunities and limitations of the use of civil resistance against corporate targets. Both campaigns follow a directed network campaign structure, enabling spontaneous and nimble development and use of grassroots, autonomous groups to target different entities using disruptive civil resistance tactics. Our empirical findings add to many years of theoretical research highlighting the link between informal groups and contentious protest activities (e.g., Carmin and Balser 2002). It appears that the directed network model offers several strengths, supporting a recent review of campaigns undertaken by NetChange (2016). They found that the use of this structure—such as in the campaign against the Keystone XL pipeline carrying oil from the Canadian oil sands mines to Nebraska—achieved both high impact and growth over longer periods of time than decentralized, spontaneous campaigns such as Occupy Wall Street and the Arab Spring.

Looking at tactics and targets, we see that civil resistance tactics are only a small minority of tactics used across the full dataset. The primary tactic used by groups active in the Stop Adani campaign is information sharing. The focus on this conventional tactic is not surprising given that Australia is a democratic country where multiple organizing and resistance avenues remain available to activists. It has been argued that activists expand beyond traditional democratic institutional channels (e.g., lawsuits, elections, lobbying, petitions) when people increasingly perceive the formal democratic system is at least partially dominated by economic and political power elites frustrating the popular will (Louis 2009). In the case of the Stop Adani campaign this holds true; continued government support for the mine appears to have pushed the campaign toward disruptive civil resistance tactics as a supplementary mechanism to create pressure on power elites who are blocking significant reform through traditional channels. Campaigns and movements that rely primarily or solely on civil resistance strategies tend to take place in more authoritarian, colonial, or dictatorial regimes where standard channels of change do not exist or are almost completely rigged (Porta and Rucht 2002). Furthermore, consequences for activists in these regimes are severe—for example, Global Witness identified the murder of 207 land and environmental defenders globally in 2017 alone (Global Witness 2018).

*The use of the directed network model achieved both high impact and growth over longer periods of time than decentralized, spontaneous campaigns.*

Both campaigns in Australia also use disruptive and creative civil resistance tactics in their activities. However, some limitations of these tactical choices can be observed. Most disruptive civil resistance tactics used in the Divestment campaign occur against educational targets. This presents a unique challenge to groups organizing these activities; they may experience high volunteer turnover and—particularly in the case of university groups—a younger demographic who may be absent during holiday periods and who experience substantial financial or social demands on their time. Given that countering the entrenched positions of those targets that have so far refused to commit to divestment will take sustained mobilization, these factors may make it difficult for grassroots groups to organize and maintain the level of disruption required to force change. In addition, the tapering off of divestment announcements means that the low hanging fruit may have been already picked, such that remaining targets need to use new tactical repertoires and approaches.

Only two groups in the Stop Adani campaign consistently use disruptive civil resistance tactics against primary or secondary targets, namely Frontline Action on Coal and Galilee Blockade. These groups are not student-centered and draw on residents of a wide range of communities in the larger region. As a result, they may experience a lower volunteer turnover than university-based groups working on the Divestment campaign. Furthermore, the Stop Adani campaign is directed toward a corporation undertaking work in a clearly defined physical location. This has enabled the development of a blockade camp to support consistent actions against the target, providing a focal point for directing human and financial resources from across Australia. In contrast, Divestment campaign volunteers have often been unable to pool resources together, with each group appearing to remain largely isolated in their efforts against a multiplicity of targets.

The nature of the target appears to lead to different outcomes as well. Despite both campaigns targeting corporate entities, those targeted by the Divestment campaign do not seem as susceptible to civil resistance tactics nor community pressure, as are entities associated with the mine. This may be due to the financial threat that mine contractors face if they become the targets of boycotts, combined with the threat of losing potential income from their narrower client base. In contrast, organizations might have thousands or even millions of clients, and investment in fossil fuels still has the potential to be financially rewarding for investors, which may make organizations more reluctant and less likely to commit to divestment. Conversely, the Stop Adani campaign has demonstrated the ability of civil resistance tactics to directly affect project work by potential contractors at their own specific worksites. This has resulted in potential contractors incurring substantial costs and delays on projects and on their daily work operations. However, in the Stop Adani campaign not all secondary targets have given in to campaign demands despite substantial disruptive and creative civil resistance tactics. There may be some unique characteristic of corporate entities who refuse to agree with campaign demands (e.g., Wagners and Siemens) that makes them less susceptible to activists' demands, whereas others capitulate fairly quickly. While we are unable to address this question with our data, further analysis could help shed light on these differential responses.

Finally, these two campaigns demonstrate a stark contrast between the outcomes of civil resistance directed against corporate targets versus governments or government entities. Analysis from the case study data indicates a higher success rate when using civil resistance tactics against corporate targets. Apart from emerging signs that local and some state governments may be prepared to announce climate emergencies or to draft supporting statements against the mine, few other wins against government have been achieved in either campaign. Although local government announcements recognizing a climate emergency indicates increased awareness of the issue, there is limited evidence that any governments are actually changing their practices or policies to reduce carbon emissions. Indeed, over the nine years that the Stop Adani campaign has progressed, the mine itself has received support from all levels of government. In addition, close connections between political powerholders in Australia and the Adani Corporation owner in India have ensured the survival of the mine proposal despite questions around its financial viability (Beresford 2019). Despite growing public opposition to the mine (Massola 2018), this situation seems consistent with Gilens and Page's (2014) research demonstrating the significant power that business interests have over government policy in contrast to citizens' lack of independent influence. While both campaigns have managed to achieve substantial successes, neither have fully challenged the substantial power of the fossil fuel industry and their continued influence in Australian politics (Knaus 2020).

These two case studies have demonstrated how civil resistance has been used by groups active in the Australian environmental movement. It builds upon the wealth of empirical data presented in Chapter 2, which we map onto the three movement frameworks in Chapter 5. Before we present these findings, however, we finally turn to an investigation into the responses these civil resistance tactics are generating from the state. Understanding these responses will provide better insight into the potential that civil resistance against climate change has for effecting change, as well as its ability to be sustained over time.

# Chapter 4: State Responses to Disruptive Civil Resistance

In the previous chapters we presented data on the civil resistance actions used by the Australian environmental movement, and more specifically climate change civil resistance tactics and campaign outcomes. The data shows a steadily increasing number of new groups over that time, particularly groups focused on climate change. The most common type of civil resistance tactics used were acts of expression, that is, events such as rallies, marches, and demonstrations. Only a small proportion of actions were disruptive acts of commission, intended to physically interfere with the regular workings of an organization or physical space. Most acts of commission involved creative activities, such as die-ins and bike swarms. There were several acts of omission, primarily due to the number of local groups engaging in the school strike for climate and divestment activities. Finally, a very small number of events were refraining acts. These predominantly occurred when events were canceled due to a campaign win or some other factor.

In this chapter we build on these insights by focusing on the occurrence and consequences of disruptive civil resistance tactics, specifically those which have generated a police response. We focus on these types of actions in order to identify how the Australian government is responding to more confrontational forms of civil resistance within a democratic political system, and to identify the tools they may be using to suppress this type of action.

In the literature examining the nature of state responses to activism, much research focuses on how the state responds to violent action (whether violence includes damage to property or physical harm to persons), or how the state uses violent responses itself (Louis and Montiel 2018). In the environmental context, research has found a large proportion of environmental protests incur violent repression, particularly when protests are undertaken by marginalized groups and concentrated in the Global South in Latin America and Asia (Poulos and Haddad 2016). Yet, there is considerable nuance involved in how these state responses may differ depending on whether they are directed at violent or nonviolent action, and whether the protest is sustained or a single event (Chenoweth, Perkoski, and Kang 2017). There is also considerable nuance around what sort of repressive responses occur in particular contexts. For example, Chenoweth and colleagues (2017) document state responses that include increased protest policing, state terror, human rights abuses, internet surveillance, and outsourcing repression to militias.

Activists and their organizations also have many ways they can respond to repression, ranging from halting protest activities to escalating their use of nonviolent or violent actions.

Repressive responses to activism can also backfire and lead to increased support for the cause when the repression is perceived as unjust or disproportionate (Martin 2015). Activists can increase the likelihood of repressive responses backfiring by using several strategies, such as exposing repressive responses, emphasizing their unjustness, and resisting intimidation where possible. Activists can also direct their efforts toward challenging the legitimacy of the state or seeking changes in policy through conventional, nonviolent, or violent actions (Cunningham 2013) and thereby undermine the ability of the state to repress activism. Of relevance to this study is evidence demonstrating how repression may occur differently in democratic and autocratic regimes (Hill and Jones 2014; Uluğ and Acar 2018). It is argued that democracies more peacefully accommodate political dissent and are thus less likely to be afflicted by violent civil conflict (for a review, see Vining 2011). In Australia, there is a relatively consistent history of largely peaceful responses to environmental activism, no recorded deaths of environmental activists in custody, and few claims of violence against activists beyond excessive police force (Branagan 2003).

Despite this, and, as we have outlined in previous chapters, there are suggestions that the Australian government has levied its power toward suppressing environmental civil resistance. For example, we have described how the Breakfree Blockade of Newcastle Coal Port in 2016 resulted in investigations of the charitable status of 350.org. In this chapter, we focus on disruptive civil resistance tactics leading to arrests, and government responses to these activities. In so doing, we can gain a deeper understanding of how the Australian government has responded to climate change civil resistance and thus identify how groups are reacting in turn.

## Investigating State Repression

The relationship between nonviolent resistance and state responses may be difficult to observe, and thus difficult to measure (Chenoweth, et al. 2017). Many organizations do not specifically state in their campaign and event communication that disruptive tactics may be used. Therefore, while we can identify some disruptive civil resistance tactics in our dataset, our data likely does not fully represent the type of tactics used as a whole. A second reason why it is difficult to measure repression is that it may be undertaken by the state or corporations out of the public eye. This is true in Australia. For example, the investigation into 350.org by the Australian Federal Government after the Breakfree Blockade was not transparent to the group or the community. These investigations were undertaken confidentially, with very little detail made available to the public, making it challenging to fully understand the scope of mechanisms used by the state to restrict civil resistance. Finally, responses such as cautions, arrests, and punitive bail conditions related to specific civil resistance tactics are also not made publicly available. While information can be obtained through Freedom of

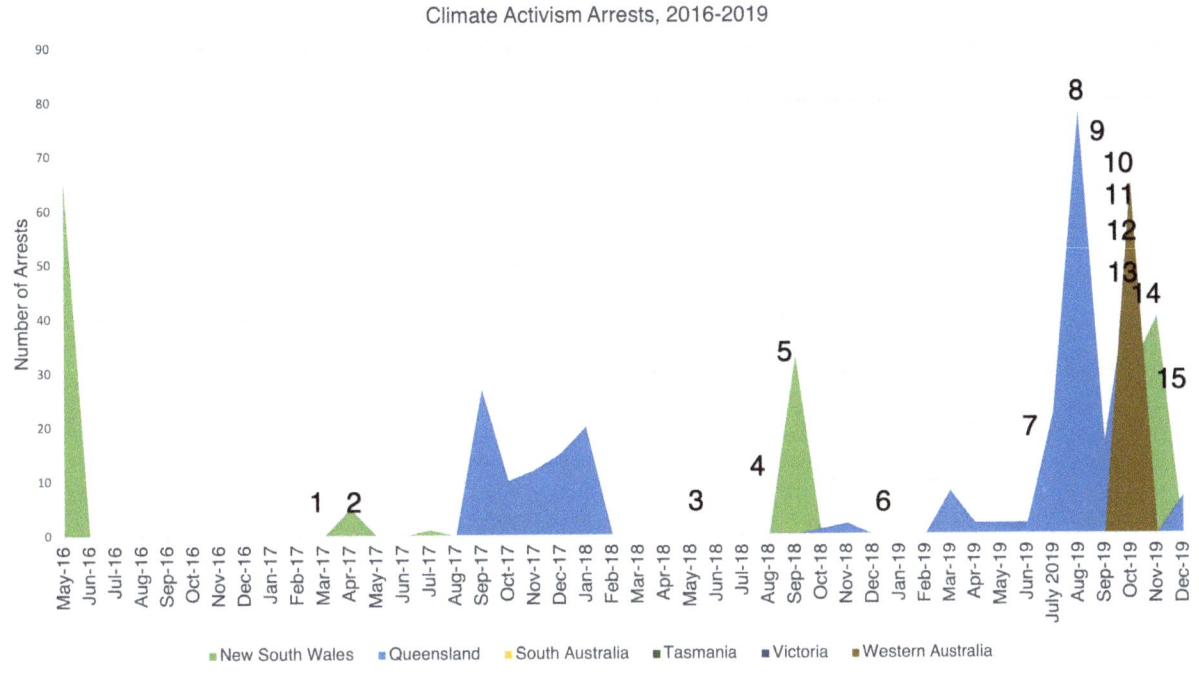

**FIGURE 18.** Climate Activism Arrests, Broken Down Across States, 2016–2019

Information (FOI) requests, this process is slow and expensive, and requests are often refused (Knass and Bassano 2019).

To overcome these limitations, we have compiled information gathered through media coverage of arrests related to climate change activism. Where available our database records the number of arrests, the location, the activist group, and the arrest charge. Very little information was available on subsequent outcomes for those arrested, although some reports highlighted fines as high as AU$10,000 for a coal train blockade (XR Aus 2019) and activists being denied bail for minor offenses (Wallan 2019). In the following section we present the findings from this data.

**Disruptive Civil Resistance Tactics and Government Responses**

Although we do not delve into arrests that are not related to climate change activism, Australia has a long history of arrests related primarily to forestry, water, and nuclear protest that preceded 2016. Figure 18 shows our analysis of media reports and indicate that a large number of arrests related to climate change activism is also occurring. We found a total of 536 arrests for climate-related activism covered in media reports between 2016 and 2019, with the earliest known arrest occurring in May 2016. Figure 18 demonstrates the clusters of arrests occurring in each Australian State between 2016 and 2019. The numbers in the figure correspond to government responses, which are listed in Table 21 (on the following page).

### Table 21. Government Responses to Disruptive Civil Resistance

| ID | DATE | RESPONSE | GOVERNMENT |
|---|---|---|---|
| 1 | 3/13/2017 | Government rushes to amend native title laws after federal court decision overrules Adani agreement. | Federal |
| 2 | 5/20/2017 | Government proposes new laws against masks at protests, with maximum penalty of 7 years for affray and 15 years for violent disorder. | Victoria |
| 3 | 6/26/2018 | New Crown Lands Management Regulation 20168 gives public officials power to direct a person to stop taking part in any gathering, meeting, or assembling. | New South Wales |
| 4 | 8/14/2018 | Government amends law to make it easier for Federal Government to call directly for military support despite wishes of state government. | Federal |
| 5 | 9/06/2018 | Push for politically active charities including Greenpeace and Australian Conservation Foundation to lose charity status. | Federal |
| 6 | 1/29/2019 | Tasmanian State Government seeks to resurrect Tasmanian anti-protest laws, seeking to institute a jail term of up to 18 months for anyone interfering with Tasmanian businesses. | Tasmania |
| 7 | 7/22/2019 | New farm trespass laws, with fines of up to AU$220,000 per person and AU$440,000 for corporations. | New South Wales |
| 8 | 8/20/2019 | New laws to be introduced into state parliament to search protesters suspected of possessing so-called "locking devices." | Queensland |
| 9 | 8/27/2019 | Brisbane City Council tries but fails to shut down protest through courts. | Brisbane City Council |
| 10 | 9/13/2019 | New laws pass making it illegal to incite others to enter farms via "carriage services" such as websites or social media. | Federal |
| 11 | 10/15/2019 | Council bars Extinction Rebellion from using council libraries and other council facilities. | Brisbane City Council |
| 12 | 10/23/2019 | Adani gets court order to restrict protester Adrian Burragubba entering traditional lands overlapping proposed coal mine. | Queensland |
| 13 | 10/24/2019 | Lock on laws pass state parliament prohibiting certain devices used by protesters. | Queensland |
| 14 | 11/1/2019 | Australian Prime Minister Morrison announces consideration of legal means to outlaw boycott campaigns. | Federal |
| 15 | 12/18/2019 | ACNC (Australian charity regulator) removes charitable status of Vegan Rising after Melbourne traffic blockade. | Federal |

The arrests we identified in this media analysis occurred in six states across four primary clusters. The first of these clusters occurred in May 2016 with 66 arrests made at the Breakfree Blockade of Newcastle Coal Port. This was followed by a series of arrests in late 2017 near the proposed Adani mine in north Queensland. Charges against activists included trespassing, interfering with a railway, contravening a police direction to move on, assault, and interfering with equipment of a vehicle. A third cluster of arrests occurred in September 2018, again related to a coal port protest in Newcastle. Finally, a fourth cluster occurred in late 2019 and were related to the Adani campaign in north Queensland, Extinction Rebellion arrests in Brisbane, and a dozen arrests in Melbourne during a mining conference. In addition to arrest-related data, we also searched online for media reports on new government legislation, proposals, or responses to climate change activism dated from the first recorded arrest. In total, 12 government responses were found, including proposals for new legislation restricting rights to protest, bans on protest devices, and investigations into select organizations' charitable status. Table 21 shows that there were a range of responses from different levels of government seeking to reduce or halt protests. The Brisbane City Council in Queensland sought to deny approval for an Extinction Rebellion protest and ban the use of its facilities for meetings by the group. At the state level, governments sought to bring in new legislation banning the right to protest on business premises (Tasmania), banning the use of lock on devices (Queensland), and banning activists' access and communications around farms and gatherings (New South Wales). Finally, the federal government used a wide variety of strategies in response to protest and threats to the mining sector. These range from amending Native Title law related to the facilitation of agreements with mining companies, threatening environmental organizations with the loss of their charitable status, and threatening bans on boycotts. No evidence was found of any government expanding citizens' rights to engage in activism or disruptive protest.

> *At the state level, governments sought to bring in new legislation banning the right to protest on business premises, banning the use of lock on devices, and banning activists' access and communications around farms and gatherings.*

While it is evident that there has been a range of responses from all levels of government attempting to repress climate civil resistance, the data on events and number of groups indicates that governments are not achieving their goal. Instead, the number of events is increasing in tandem with the substantial emergence of new groups. There are three features of this development that are interesting. First, almost all new groups appear to be grassroots, with no formal legal structure. This eliminates the power held by the state to restrict their activities through revoking their charitable status. Second, disruptive protest appears to be increasing rather than decreasing. This may be due to the urgency of climate action, but it also aligns with scholarship suggesting that increased repression can lead to increased disruptive protest (Louis, et al. 2020; see also Meyer 2004; Tilly 1978). Described as "backfire" (Martin 2015) and "backlash" (see Louis, et al. 2020), this occurs when state repression—particularly when violent—can fuel increased radical nonviolent and violent action. However, our data shows no evidence of a violent state response which could help explain the growth of groups due to backlash against the government. In fact, analysis by Martin (2015) on the dynamics of backfire indicates that the use of official channels (such as the courts) and devaluing the target (such as negative media coverage of protesters) to suppress activism may actually reduce backlash. It is thus not clear whether the growth of activist groups is generated by backlash against these state responses or is instead explained by other mechanisms, such as growing outrage around the lack of action on climate change. Future research could build upon our data to focus on the effects of backlash that violence against climate change civil resistance groups and other audiences can generate.

Finally, these data indicate that arrests in north Queensland have occurred regularly over three years. These arrests are all related to the Stop Adani campaign and are targeted at the Adani Corporation or their mine site contractors. The persistence of these arrests indicate that the state has so far been unable to completely suppress localized, targeted, disruptive civil resistance through legislative means. It also suggests that this persistent disruptive action may be more sustainable for activists, in contrast to the bursts of arrests occurring around the Breakfree Blockade, the International Mining and Resources conference, and Rebellion Week in Brisbane. The reasons for activists' resilience in the face of the arrests in Queensland remains to be established and are worthy of future research.

## Insights and Key Findings on State Responses

In this chapter we have presented data gathered through an online media search on government responses and arrests for climate change civil resistance actions. Our data demonstrates that peaks of arrests have occurred at key moments between 2016 and 2019, namely the Breakfree Blockade in May 2016, northern Queensland arrests in early 2017 with the formation of the Adani blockade camp, and the Extinction Rebellion "Rebellion Week" protests in October 2019. Throughout this period, smaller numbers of arrests have also taken place, consistently in northern Queensland for the Stop Adani campaign.

In response to this activism, all levels of government have attempted to restrict the use of disruptive civil resistance tactics. This is not isolated to this period, however. Australian governments have consistently attempted to use legislative means to restrict rights to protest (Paris 2019). However, it appears that none of the attempts at repression within the 2016–2019 period have resulted in substantial reduction of protest activity. Our data suggests several explanations for this. First, the growth of new groups has occurred almost exclusively in the grassroots arena. These groups remain informal and are likely to have low financial resources—characteristics which have been linked to engagement in more confrontational actions (Dalton, Recchia, and Rohrschneider 2003).

Although the grassroots nature of these groups means they are unable to acquire organizational and financial resources, this constraint is overcome through two mechanisms. Strategizing and planning may be undertaken entirely by volunteers (e.g., Extinction Rebellion), or these organizational tasks are outsourced to professional organizations with charitable status that do not themselves engage (nor advocate for their supporters to engage) in civil resistance tactics. Groups with greater financial resources have also challenged laws in the courts, as seen with the successful overthrow of the Tasmanian anti-protest laws (Howie 2017). Our findings indicate that strong networks between groups operating in different movement niches may be a powerful way to overcome efforts by the state to suppress protest.

Groups have also sidestepped government attempts to restrict protest through other means, such as through evolving disruptive tactics. New disruptive techniques mean that the Queensland "protest devices" law, while argued to be bad legislation (Guille 2019), was rendered ineffective almost immediately by activists who adopted new technologies which had not been listed in the old legislation (Wordsworth 2019). The use of novel civil resistance tactics such as traffic swarms by Extinction Rebellion (groups of individuals that block traffic but disperse rapidly to changing locations) also ensured that activists could achieve their tactical goals and leave before arrests occurred.

Although this data yields rich insights into how movements can change and respond dynamically to repression, it must be noted that this data has some limitations. First, it is highly likely that substantially more arrests have occurred and that the state may have used other forms of suppression which are not so easily detected. These could include the use of surveillance and arrests occurring outside the media's eye (Hamilton 2014), as well as the use of agent provocateurs to incite or implicate activists in incriminating actions. Second, the challenge that activist groups have in promoting their events without explicitly advocating for disruptive action makes identification of these events methodologically difficult. As a result, it is not possible to accurately track any specific changes in civil resistance tactics over time.

Despite these challenges, the data indicates that the climate change movement in Australia has been able to adapt to the range of repressive responses from the government. The movement has achieved this through flexibility in disruptive civil resistance tactics and the effective use of organizations with greater financial resources to challenge legislation and assist with strategy and planning. The existence of the Stop Adani camp in northern Queensland appears to enable continuous, low-level disruptive action against the mine to continue locally. To the extent that repressive responses have been seen to be illegitimate overreach—not only by activists but by the broader community—the state actions may also have increased the human and financial resources of the movement by broadening the support and volunteer base. However, our data is unable to speak clearly to this dynamic, and future research should explore these processes empirically.

In the following chapter we consider the extent to which data presented in previous chapters aligns with the three frameworks presented in Chapter 1. These movement frameworks can help to identify areas of strength and opportunity for the climate movement to continue to grow and increase their power in order to achieve meaningful action against climate change in the future.

# Chapter 5: Mapping Climate Change Civil Resistance onto Movement Frameworks

Throughout this monograph we have traced the issues, tactics, and outcomes of groups engaging in civil resistance to create meaningful action on climate change. In this chapter we integrate our findings and map them onto the three frameworks introduced in Chapter 1: The Great Turning model (Macy 2007), the Climate Insurgency model (Brecher 2015), and the political process model (Tilly 1978; McAdam 1982). Each framework is composed of components linked to movement emergence and outcomes. The following sections present the key questions for each of the framework components posed in Chapter 1, alongside the findings from our data.

## Macy's Great Turning

The Great Turning model argues that three components are required to help sustain the action needed to address our environmental and climate crisis. Table 22 summarizes the components, data, evidence, and outcome of mapping our findings against the model. The "Outcome" column refers to our assessment of the degree to which our data demonstrates that these components are actually occurring. We elaborate on these outcomes below.

### Table 22. Mapping Data onto the Components of the Great Turning

| COMPONENT | DATA | EVIDENCE | OUTCOME |
|---|---|---|---|
| Holding actions, resisting | Civil resistance actions | Large number of actions being promoted, particularly rallies | ✓ |
| | Legal and regulatory campaign goals | High number of campaigns targeting regulation and politicians | ✓ |
| Creating alternative structures | Social creative actions | Growing number of these actions are promoted | ✓ |
| | Building alternative groups | Some new alternative groups and alliances are emerging | ✓ |
| Shift in consciousness and values | No data available | NA | ? |

**Component 1: Holding Actions, Resisting**

Our data demonstrates a substantial level of engagement in actions across groups focused on a wide range of environmental issues. Although we are unable to ascertain the number of events that actually took place, the size of the event dataset (27,934 unique promoted events) and the civil resistance tactics within it (3,705) indicate that the movement is holding actions and demonstrating resistance, as Macy argues, is required to drive the Great Turning. It is evident that across the dataset most events are related to information sharing; it is possible that these events may also be contributing to increasing individual and group ability to take action as well as helping to shift consciousness and values (Component 3).

**Component 2: Creating Alternative Structures**
While challenging to identify across our dataset, evidence exists that work is being undertaken to build alternative structures through the emergence of grassroots local groups. It is unclear whether most of these grassroots groups also focus on creating alternative structures. However, groups such as Transition Towns, sustainability groups, and Extinction Rebellion are active in building local resilience and support.

**Component 3: Shift in Consciousness and Values**
Our data is unable to speak directly to this component, however, there are indications from other data that a shift in values is slowly taking place. For example, on one hand, there are some positive signs that people are more aware than ever of climate change and biodiversity loss and that pro-environmental values are increasingly taught in the Australian education system (Karena 2010) and integrated into religious leaders' advocacy (e.g., via the Australian Religious Response to Climate Change organization[10]). Green political movements now attract millions of voters worldwide and received 10.4 percent of the vote in the 2019 Australian federal election. However, it is clear that the shift in values is not as large or universal as is needed. Growth continues to be the main metric of economic success (Lange, Wodon, and Carey 2018) and "biospheric values" (Bouman and Steg 2019) are not ubiquitous. While a recent Australian poll found that 79 percent of respondents were concerned about climate change (The Australia Institute 2020)—in line with polling data suggesting a steady rise in concern about climate change since 2012 (Lowy Institute n.d.)—other evidence suggests that Australians may not connect environmental threats to specific places like the Great Barrier Reef with the need for action on climate change (Dean, Gulliver, and Wilson 2021). Future research should chart changes in consciousness and values in more detail and consider mechanisms that increase or slow the trajectory of change.

**Summary of the Great Turning Model**
In summary, our data enables mapping of environmental movement activities against the Great Turning component related to "holding actions/resisting" alone. A substantial proportion of events promoted by environmental groups use a range of civil resistance tactics to attempt to force change. In addition, while our data is not able to assess the extent to which

---

10   See **www.arrcc.org.au**.

alternative structures are emerging, our findings suggest that groups are focused intensely on information sharing activities, as well as building organizations such as the New Economy Network and Transition Towns Network. We suggest, therefore, that the movement does demonstrate characteristics aligned with the Great Turning. However, future research could gather empirical evidence more closely aligned with these components to investigate this question in more depth and to test how activists relate to each component and whether or how they have chosen to address them.

## Brecher's Climate Insurgency

Jeremy Brecher argued that an effective response to climate change will require a climate insurgency (as defined by Brecher as a rapid, mass engagement in nonviolent action challenging the legitimacy of existing state and corporate authority). This insurgency needs mass participation in direct action and a focus on litigation to challenge the legitimacy of the state. Brecher stipulates the need for individuals to self-organize and deisolate (defined by Brecher as joining together in grassroots groups, and framing climate action toward changing systems rather than personal behaviors, respectively). Brecher argues these behaviors are required to build the organizational structures needed to implement the insurgency. We mapped our data onto these four aspects, as shown in Table 23.

### Table 23. Mapping Data onto the Components of the Climate Insurgency

| COMPONENT | DATA | EVIDENCE | OUTCOME |
|---|---|---|---|
| An insurgency of civil resistance | Civil resistance actions | Large number of actions being promoted, but far less than required for insurgency | x |
| Legal arguments and litigation | Campaign targets and goals | High number of campaigns targeting regulation and politicians. | ✓ |
| | | Limited evidence of litigation used as a tactic | x |
| Self-organization and deisolation | Number and growth of local groups | Substantial growth of local sub-groups affiliated with XR and Stop Adani | ✓ |
| | Categories of campaign goals | Most campaigns target systems or institutions, rather than individuals | ✓ |

**Component 1: An Insurgency of Civil Resistance**
Brecher argues that addressing the climate crisis requires mass engagement in civil resistance tactics, particularly disruptive tactics. Our data suggests, however, that while civil resistance is taking place, the majority of events undertaken by environmental organizations are conventional activities such as information sharing events. Second, disruptive civil resistance is often highly localized (for example, the ongoing blockade at the Adani coal mine in northern Queensland). Third, our data suggests that ongoing civil resistance may be difficult to sustain:

as demonstrated in Chapter 4, arrests occur in short waves in different locations rather than continuously in the same locations. Further, most arrests are linked to the Stop Adani campaign or similar clearly defined targets such as coal mines and banks. Large scale mass disruptive civil resistance against governments does not appear to be occurring. Furthermore, attempts to engage in large-scale resistance (e.g., Extinction Rebellion civil resistance tactics) have met with a range of repressive responses by the government. As such, the civil resistance currently shown by our data is not likely to cause transformational change according to the first component of Brecher's model.

**Component 2: Legal Arguments and Litigation**
Across our dataset there is little indication that groups are promoting activities that relate to legal challenges. However, we do see that some larger organizations such as the Australian Conservation Foundation and the Environmental Defenders Office focus on this form of tactic, particularly in relation to environmental conditions of coal and coal seam gas mining projects, corporate disclosures around climate risk, and litigation against specific climate polluting companies (Korbel 2019). In addition, some environmental groups have launched successful legal challenges against coal expansion plans, and Australia currently has the second highest number (after the United States) of climate-related cases before the courts (Bell-James 2020). More than half of climate change campaigns in our dataset target politicians and other political entities.

Despite this, the Australian legal and political context may present a significant barrier to the unfolding of a climate insurgency via changes to legislation. There are significant challenges in creating new legal and constitutional frameworks within Australia's existing legislative system. Although support is growing through the development of the Australian Centre for the Rights of Nature (https://rightsofnature.org.au), groups in our study population seldom took legal actions or ran campaigns demanding changes to the existing legislative system. This may be due to the limitations of the Australia legal framework to adequately address climate change, as well as the high cost incurred on groups engaging in legal tactics (Trenorden 2014).

**Component 3: Self-Organization and Deisolation**
As highlighted above, our data indicates that a rapid growth of grassroots, self-organizing groups is occurring within the movement, although we are unable to determine the extent to which these groups can engage in sustained activities or persist over time. Maintaining groups over a longer term, particularly grassroots groups, is notoriously difficult due to challenges in retaining volunteers, obtaining financial resources, building strong networks, and managing ideological disputes (Feola and Nunes 2014).

Brecher highlights the importance of deisolation in building the local, grassroots connections required to create and sustain a climate insurgency. Considering that most new groups that have emerged over the past five years have been grassroots, we suggest that our data indicates that deisolation is occurring. In addition, although many campaigns focus on changing individual behaviors (e.g., reducing meat consumption), the majority of climate change campaign targets and goals focus on changing systems (e.g., banning coal seam gas mining). From the vantage of Brecher's model, these are encouraging changes.

**Summary of the Climate Insurgency Model**

In conclusion, some of the components identified in Brecher's Climate Insurgency model are evident. However, Brecher's central point is the need for activists to engage in legal arguments and litigation to challenge the legitimacy of state responses. Australia lacks federal laws controlling emissions, and it has no civil rights guarantees in its constitution, unlike the United States (Stanton 2019). Academic research indicates that a collective action approach to driving climate action using legislative methods in Australia is thus unlikely to deliver action on reducing emissions (Peel 2007), although it may hold hope for the future as international cases build legal precedents supporting citizens' right to a climate-safe future (Baxter 2017). Despite this potential barrier, other aspects of Brecher's Climate Insurgency model appear to be used by the climate change movement in Australia.

## Political Process Model

In this section we consider the extent to which our data maps onto the three components of the political process model: political opportunities, mobilizing structures, and framing, as shown in Table 24.

### Table 24. Mapping Data onto the Components of the Political Process Model

| COMPONENT | ASPECT | EVIDENCE | OUTCOME |
|---|---|---|---|
| **Political opportunities** | Being heard in the political arena | Many campaigns targeting political entities achieve success | ✓ |
| | Capitalizing on political changes | Mixed success in election campaigns | x |
| | Finding new allies | No evidence this is occurring | ? |
| **Mobilizing structures** | Local, grassroots groups | Substantial growth of local groups | ✓ |
| | Building coalitions and alliances | Growth of directed network campaigns | ✓ |
| | Sustaining activism | Some groups unable to sustain online presence | x |
| **Framing** | Using different and numerous frames | Four different communication climate change frames | ✓ |
| | Identification of an antagonist | Antagonist identified in some campaigns, but not all | ? |

**Component 1: Political Opportunities**
The data indicates that the movement is to some extent being heard in the political arena: 48 percent of the 75 climate change campaigns aimed at political targets achieved full or partial success. Despite this success, Australia was the first country to remove a carbon pricing mechanism and remains one of the highest emitters per capita, with fossil fuel mining continuing apace. Thus, political successes are not translating into meaningful emissions reductions.

The second aspect of this component we consider is whether the movement is capitalizing on political changes, which in the Australian context occur during election campaigns (as opposed to other radical social, political, or economic upheavals). Campaigns were run during the 2018 federal election and various state elections, but few positive policy outcomes were obtained. Few other political changes have occurred (e.g., no regime change or civil war) and thus there appears to have been limited opportunities for activists to capitalize on political changes (e.g., such as a change of political party in government). Some evidence of localized success such as climate emergency declarations and divestment commitments from local governments suggest that the movement may be capitalizing on political opportunities at the local level given the entrenched position of the federal government. At the time of writing, the extent to which the movement has been able to respond to political changes associated with the disruptive 2019–2020 Australian bushfire season and the COVID-19 pandemic is unknown.

The final aspect of the political opportunities component is the ability to find new allies. Our data does not clearly speak to the extent that the movement has found new allies within the political arena. However, across the movement many actions and campaigns have asked businesses to support climate change action through actions such as divestment commitments. In addition, increasing numbers of businesses are supporting climate action—for example, the Business Council of Australia and the growing network of social enterprises and businesses focused on sustainability. A project for future research would be to explore the formation and impact of environmental groups attracting new constituencies, such as more conservative voters, workers in fossil fuel industries, and new religious, regional, or business partners.

**Component 2: Mobilizing Structures**
There appears to have been a rapid change of mobilizing structures over the past five years, with the substantial growth of grassroots groups connected through directed network campaigns or alliances. These groups are very active. Our data suggests that larger groups have the resources available to design campaign strategy and undertake high-cost tactics such as legal actions. Grassroots groups are likely to have a high level of volunteer resources given this increase in activity. It is unclear whether these grassroots groups have support from elites.

There also appears to be a shift toward increasing coalitions. The data indicates that over the past fifty years the movement has been shifting from formal organizations to directed network campaigns, where hundreds of new informal grassroots groups are linked to central groups which help to design and organize campaign strategy. Many groups engage in shared campaigns (e.g., Stop Adani), indicating the presence of coalitions sharing resources and strategies. Our data also indicates that the climate change movement in Australia is pursuing multiple goals across multiple targets and achieving a great number of them. At the same time, the extent to which the environmental movement connects across the political spectrum—or even with other movements in Australia, such as movements for women's rights, Indigenous peoples, or unions—has not been mapped.

The final consideration of effective mobilizing structures is the ability of the movement to support sustained activism. The vast numbers of emerging grassroots groups, ranging from semi-autonomous (e.g., Stop Adani and AYCC groups) to fully autonomous (e.g., Extinction Rebellion), indicates the ability of the movement to engage in sustained organizing. However, the longer-term survival of these groups remains to be seen, particularly since this growth was not observed in all groups (e.g., not with 350.org groups). Our event data demonstrates that sustained civil resistance is occurring, including disruptive civil resistance taking place in northern Queensland on the Stop Adani campaign. This indicates significant resources have been acquired to support activists in the area.

**Component 3: Framing**

How the issue of climate change is framed in communication channels is very important. Consistent with this model, framing in this monograph refers to the particular words and concepts linked to the issue of climate change. Effective communication to mobilize supporters requires the use of multiple frames which identify a clear antagonist.

Topic analysis of website text indicates that climate change communication by environmental groups in Australia is associated with four frames and that the most common words associated with these frames suggest some of the problems (e.g., coal, reef, company), as well as solutions (e.g., energy policy, campaign, action). However, one comment that might be made is that the climate justice frame, despite its prevalence in climate change activism in other countries, does not emerge clearly from our analysis. Future research could examine whether the frames of successful campaigns differ from those of unsuccessful campaigns and, if so, how.

Although it is difficult to ascertain whether the framing clearly identifies an antagonist, our data indicates a high prevalence of words associated with coal mining, Adani, and the financial sector. In addition, our data shows that many groups focused on mining have a clear antagonist identifiable through the group name—for example, CSG Free Sydney. Other group names indicate other features such as the action required ("Lock the Gate"), the location of the issue and action ("Galilee Blockade"), or the issue ("Clean Energy for Eternity"). Overall, though, it was often unclear in either the group name or event data who the target was. Similarly, just under 10 percent of climate change campaigns did not state who the target was. Thus, activists could increase the mobilization potential of their communication by ensuring that they offer multiple frames for issues and clearly identify the antagonist they are seeking to influence.

**Summary for Political Process Model**

The results from mapping our data onto the political process model indicates that the climate change movement in Australia is particularly strong in its diverse range of mobilizing structures and multiple framings of the issue of climate change. Although the movement appears to be capitalizing on the political opportunities available to it and achieving some political successes, these do not appear to be translated into changing the stance of the federal government on climate change.

## Insights from the Application of These Models

The findings we have presented in this chapter indicate that the Australian climate change movement, including those engaged in civil resistance within it, has many of the proposed characteristics required to effect environmental change. In many areas, it is showing substantial success. It is capitalizing on multiple avenues for engaging in the political process while also targeting businesses and specific emissions causing projects. It has also developed a highly nimble, flexible mobilizing structure possessing a strong foundation of volunteer resources and framing many of its climate change civil resistance tactics as solutions-based. New groups building grassroots alternatives are emerging, alongside new actions such as climate emergency declarations and divestment commitments. These features indicate that the movement has potential to continue achieving success. In the following section, we use the findings of our research to inform a non-exhaustive list of recommendations for activists, researchers, and external parties.

# Chapter 6: Takeaways for Specific Groups

## Activists and Civil Society Groups

**Build strong alliances between local grassroots groups**

This study demonstrates how grassroots groups connecting through directed network campaigns or other alliances can hold significant power to effect change. The benefits of this mobilization structure (as shown by the Stop Adani and Extinction Rebellion organizational structures) are twofold: First, it enables centralized groups to efficiently devise and disseminate information and resources. Second, a centralized structure also provides autonomy for local groups to choose the events they have the capacity and interest to organize. However, it is important to note that our data is correlational and cross-sectional, and we do not have clear evidence on directions of causality and how tactical effectiveness changes based on the dynamics among organizations and authorities' responses. Despite the benefits of this structure, it is also vulnerable to pressure. Given their dependency on local volunteers, grassroots groups may mobilize but then collapse quickly. Thus, activists and civil society groups should aim to support projects that connect grassroots groups together while centralizing campaign planning. For example, a small group of activists might take responsibility to monitor the big picture of the national policy environment, to research issues, and to create and share campaign materials such as tactical mapping plans and communication materials with local groups. These materials can then be locally adapted, and local groups can report information on successes or challenges. The data indicates that this will deliver other benefits as well: enabling climate change activism to be framed around local communities and local needs, and fostering more local engagement in the political process, thereby potentially avoiding repressive government responses. In addition, nurturing local grassroots groups will help build the alternative structures and systems that Macy argues is critical to achieving the Great Turning and Brecher points out is critical to facilitating deisolation. In doing so, these localized groups may offer an effective response to our environmental crisis.

**Target opponents and their allies while using different and changing tactical approaches**

This study points to the success of local, connected grassroots groups implementing multiple actions against primary and secondary targets using a diversity of tactical approaches (as shown in the two case studies). Although targeting allies of opponents may not deliver overall campaign success, it can cause delay and financial cost to opponents (such as the Adani company), while building momentum and a record of success (e.g., the Divestment campaign). The importance of this is seen most clearly in the civil resistance actions directed against secondary targets in the Stop Adani campaign. These secondary targets are entities such as banks, insurance companies, and contractors, all of whom are critical stakeholders for the Adani company in their quest to build the mine. Some successes against secondary targets were achieved within a week of organizing civil resistance against them (e.g., Greyhound buses canceled their contract with Adani within seven days of publication of the contract). Many of these successful outcomes were achieved using diverse tactics. For example, while groups involved in the Divestment campaign did use disruptive civil resistance tactics, they engaged in thousands of other conventional tactics such as education, training, and outreach to the general public.

In addition, our data indicates that changing tactical repertoires may enable groups to continue to engage in civil resistance despite attempts to repress this activism (e.g., through new laws, see Chapter 5). The emergence of new civil resistance tactics by School Strike for Climate groups (namely, strikes) and Extinction Rebellion (e.g., die-ins, swarms, and flash mobs) suggests that tactical innovation may both attract new supporters as well as introduce new challenges for authorities and opponents to manage. While these new civil resistance repertoires paint a picture of an innovative movement, it is important to also note that throughout the period studied in this monograph (June 2010 to February 2020), all groups across the dataset combined these actions with the consistent promotion of information sharing events. Thus, although our data highlights the importance of climate change civil resistance in the broader environmental movement, it also demonstrates the importance of integrating civil resistance tactics with a multitude of other conventional tactics such as informing the public and working to create change within institutional channels.

**Ensure campaigns and actions clearly communicate the target and an achievable goal**
Our third takeaway for activists and civil society groups relates to the need for clear messaging and campaign targeting. Clear framing that identifies the problem, the antagonist, and the solution is an important aspect of successful movement framing (Polletta 2008). In our data, a very large range of events and civil resistance tactics were identified. However, for almost half of civil resistance tactics it was difficult to ascertain who the target of the action was, and the solution that the activists wished them to enact. Many campaigns did not identify a measurable goal. Given that communication of success is important for helping motivate people to mobilize for the cause, campaign designers should ensure that their activities enable multiple opportunities for demonstrating success. In addition, clear messaging around targets and demands can help ensure clear and consistent messaging as well as potentially reduce the potential for community backlash against activists. For example, recent Extinction Rebellion protests and protests during the Mining Conference in Melbourne (both in October

2019) led to accusations that tactics targeting the broader population can be counterproductive and damage the cause (Molloy 2019). The community may be more willing to support or mobilize for the cause if message framing immediately conveys who the target is (of an event or campaign), what the target is asked to do, and whether that goal is achievable.

## Academics and Researchers

**Compile, use, and disseminate empirical datasets
on characteristics of environmental activism and its outcomes**
Although this monograph highlights the substantial body of research that has been developed over the past fifty years on the emergence and outcomes of nonviolent movements, there remains a significant gap in research comparing characteristics of campaigns with their outcomes. As a result, there is still much to learn about what specific characteristics of campaigns differ between successful and unsuccessful civil resistance efforts. Our recommendations for academics and researchers are therefore to compile, use, and disseminate more empirical datasets on environmental collective action gathered from countries around the world, alongside continued work developing datasets on campaign outcomes. The reach of internet communication and online technology now enables more detailed investigation of the links between campaigns, tactics, and outcomes. Given these resources, it is possible to imagine a replication of the present analyses in every national environmental movement context or the global context at large. Furthering this work would have substantial applied benefit to activists and their allies around the world, particularly in identifying opportunities for under-resourced regional and local groups to receive assistance and support.

**Bring together different disciplines and levels of analysis**
Despite the substantial body of research that has been developed on civil resistance campaigns and movements, a general comment is that the levels of analysis are not drawn together across disciplines to connect the psychology of individuals, the social psychology and sociology of groups, and the history, economics, and politics of societies. Furthermore, our data demonstrates that it is important to consider outcomes of the movement as a whole, as well as the detailed characteristics of groups and the campaigns they organize. To capture the interplay across levels of analysis, theoretical models of individual environmental decision-making (Fielding and Hornsey 2016; Fritsche, et al. 2017) should be connected with analyses of environmental political polarization (Hornsey 2020), backfire (Martin 2015), and integrated models of sustained economic and political transformation such as the Political Process model (McAdam 1982; Tilly 1978; see also Louis, et al. 2020). Given that the incentive structures of academia famously reward disciplinary silos, new mechanisms may be needed to enable these connections. For example, visionary editors could consider commissioning

regular interdisciplinary integrative reviews of research relating to effective environmental resistance campaigns and movements and their actions. Conferences and symposia on successful environmental actions—including conventional and civil resistance tactics—could be funded, offering the opportunity for remote presentations and online attendance to break free of the costs of international travel and also helping reduce travel-related carbon footprints. Blogs or websites might be set up to draw together and profile interdisciplinary scholars' work. And importantly, editors, reviewers, and scholars of environmental activism must together transition toward open science. This will allow publication of failures to replicate, help to disseminate research that is unable to identify consistent or significant findings, and better collect data to increase our understanding of how backfire might occur and how it can be used to further mobilization goals. Without these mechanisms, the pace of scholarly progress will be unnecessarily slowed.

**Investigate links between campaign goals, outcomes, and greenhouse gas emissions reductions**

Further research is required on the connection between successful campaign outcomes and measurable reductions in greenhouse gas emissions. Despite the success of climate change civil resistance demonstrated in our empirical data, these outcomes do not seem to be substantively affecting Australia's response to climate change, which is one of the worst in the world's 20 largest economies (Climate Transparency 2019). However, the lack of a comparison country or control conditions means that based on the present analysis, we cannot know whether the environmental movement in Australia has slowed the pace of emissions growth, had no impact at all, or perversely even increased it, compared to what would have occurred if no activism had been conducted. Most successful climate change outcomes identified in our dataset were not directly linked to emissions reduction (e.g., divestment and new policy frameworks), and those that were (e.g., stopping a coal mining project) required long-term sustained mobilization. Investigating which campaigns (and campaign organizational structures) most consistently lead to measurable reductions in emissions is thus in need of urgent attention.

## External Actors: The Public and the International Community

**Direct funding and other support to centralized organizations that sustain local grassroots nonviolent activist groups**

Our data indicates that while the climate change movement is capable of effecting change through grassroots activism, it is most successful when either supported through organizations with funding, or through directed network campaigns with a core group offering centralized support. This mobilization structure enables funding to be directed to organizations best able to support grassroots groups. It can also enable centralized coordination of support such as training and other capacity-building activities that assist in building more effective leadership, improve coordination across groups, and strengthen capacity to withstand repression. In addition, it limits local groups' vulnerability to government attacks on the right to advocate and promote protest (particularly protest involving disruptive civil resistance), given that many grassroots groups have no formal structure or financial dependency on the government. Our data indicates that funding and support for the climate movement is fruitfully directed toward these centralized groups to use in projects supporting grassroots mobilization, training, and capacity building. In addition, our data demonstrates the importance of supporting local grassroots groups to emerge from within local communities and directly affect change. Thus, international supporters should aim to support local groups rather than supplant them, and to funnel resources into centralized organizations such as the Stop Adani Alliance or 350.org, which emerge organically within the countries themselves.

**Target multinational corporations operating in the Global South while framing climate change as a global environmental injustice issue**

Finally, our data demonstrates the effectiveness of targeting corporate behaviors, whether in blocking projects, delaying their construction, or undermining the financial support structures that enable detrimental projects to continue. Our data also indicates that the Australian climate change movement is achieving this effectively in a context where political policy changes have been regularly stymied. We suggest that this strategy can also be effective in other nations. For example, as climate change will disproportionately affect the Global South, external actors can support activists in developing countries through pressuring multinational companies operating in these locations as well as richer nations such as Australia. This is particularly important in the Global South where much environmental activism is underpinned by concepts of environmental injustice. The international community could look to support localized activism that highlights the interaction of environmental degradation and economic, political, and social inequality. Accordingly, international supporters should ensure that efforts are not made to impose solutions on communities; instead, they should help communities build their own capacities to drive environmental change. This support can be given through financial donations to grassroots organizations working to build sustainable economic and environmental systems in the Global South, or centralized professional organizations working to support them. It can also be done through amplifying stories of those who fight against environmental injustice in other nations.

## Final Remarks

Across the globe increasing numbers of activists are rising up to demand that meaningful, urgent action is taken to reduce greenhouse gas emissions and curb the worst projected effects of climate change. In doing so, the climate change movement has gained international media attention, built a complex and sophisticated network of international actors, and sustained a wide diversity of civil resistance tactics. In this monograph we have used the Australian climate change movement as a case study to investigate what this civil resistance looks like and what it can achieve. Our data shows that the climate change movement in Australia is grassroots in nature, diverse, growing quickly, and achieving substantial success. It is using a vibrant and evolving repertoire of civil resistance tactics designed to mobilize and create change. As such, this monograph demonstrates the great promise climate change activism holds for driving the urgent action needed to effectively address our collective climate crisis.

Yet many unanswered questions also remain. Given the rapid emergence of the climate change movement, we know little about the effectiveness of its civil resistance tactics targeting diverse entities, nor the potential the movement has to achieve its goals in different political, social, and economic contexts. The authors' aspiration is that this work provides guidance for activists and supporters engaged in activism in the present moment. However, we also hope it prompts increased empirical analysis of the characteristics and outcomes of climate change-related civil resistance at a range of scales and contexts. We urgently need to better understand the causal links between civil resistance and outcomes, the effects civil resistance can have on different targets, and the extent to which responses by these targets drive measurable reductions in greenhouse gas emissions. Given that every year of rising greenhouse gases further imperils the future of countless species dependent on a livable planet, this analysis is critical to help identify the most efficient and effective strategies for driving change in the limited time we have left.

# References

**Abrash,** Abigail, and Danny Kennedy. "Repressive Mining in West Papua." In *Moving Mountains: Communities Confront Mining and Globalisation*, edited by Geoffrey Russell Evans, James Goodman, and Nina Lansbury, 59–74. Australia: Oxford Press; London: Zed Books, 2002).

**Abrash Walton,** Abigail. "Fossil Fuel Divestment: The Power of Positively Deviant Leadership for Catalyzing Climate Action and Financing Clean Energy." In *Evolving Leadership for Collective Wellbeing: Lessons for Implementing the United Nations Sustainable Development Goals*, edited by Seana Lowe Steffen and Jamie Rezmovits, with Shanah Trevenna and Shana Rappaport. Bingley: Emerald Publishing Limited, 2018a.

**Abrash Walton,** Abigail. "Positive Deviance and Behavior Change: A Research Methods Approach for Understanding Fossil Fuel Divestment." *Energy Research & Social Science* 45 (2018b): 235–249.

**Amenta,** Edwin. *When Movements Matter: The Townsend Plan and the Rise of Social Security* (Vol. 99): Princeton: Princeton University Press, 2008.

**Andrews,** Kenneth T., and Bob Edwards. "Advocacy Organizations in the U.S. Political Process." *Annual Review of Sociology* 30 (2004): 479–506. **https://doi.org/10.1146/annurev.soc.30.012703.110542**.

**Ansar,** Atif, Ben Caldecott, and James Tilbury. *Stranded Assets and the Fossil Fuel Divestment Campaign: What Does Divestment Mean for the Valuation of Fossil Fuel Assets?* Oxford: Stranded Assets Programme, Smith School of Enterprise and the Environment, 2013.

**Australian** Government. *Charities, Elections and Advocacy.* Australian Charities and Not-for-profits Commission, April 2016.

**Ayling,** Julie, and Neil Gunningham. "Non-State Governance and Climate Policy: The Fossil Fuel Divestment Movement." *Climate Policy* 17, no. 2 (2017): 131–149. **http://dx.doi.org/10.1080/14693062.2015.1094729**.

**Baker,** Nick. "The Recent History of Australia's Climate Change Wars." *SBS News*, January 23, 2020. **https://www.sbs.com.au/news/the-recent-history-of-australia-s-climate-change-wars**.

**Bandura,** Albert. "Guide for Constructing Self-Efficacy Scales." In *Self-Efficacy Beliefs of Adolescents*, edited by Tim Urdan and Frank Pajares, 307–337. Greenwich, CT: Information Age Publishing, 2006.

**Barr,** Stewart, and Justine Pollard. "Geographies of Transition: Narrating Environmental Activism in an Age of Climate Change and 'Peak Oil.'" *Environment and Planning A: Economy and Space*, 49, no. 1 (2017): 47–64.

**Bartkowski,** Maciej. "Do Civil Resistance Movements Advance Democratization?" *Minds of the Movement*, September 27, 2017. **https://www.nonviolent-conflict.org/blog_post/civil-resistance-movements-advance-democratization/**.

**Bartkowski,** Maciej, and Hardy Merriman. "Civil Resistance." *Oxford Bibliographies.* Oxford: Oxford University Press, 2016.

**Beeson,** Mark, and Matt McDonald. (2013). "The Politics of Climate Change in Australia." *Australian Journal of Politics and History* 59, no. 3 (2013): 331–348. **http://doi.org/10.1111/ajph.12019**.

**Beer,** Michael. *Civil Resistance Tactics in the 21st Century.* Washington: ICNC Press, 2021.

**Bell-James,** Justine. "These Young Queenslanders Are Taking on Clive Palmer's Coal Company and Making History for Human Rights." *The Conversation.* May 18, 2020. https://theconversation.com/these-young-queenslanders-are-taking-on-clive-palmers-coal-company-and-making-history-for-human-rights-138732.

**Benford,** Robert D., and David A. Snow. "Framing Processes and Social Movements: An Overview and Assessment." *Annual Review of Sociology* 26, no. 1 (2000): 611–639.

**Beresford,** Quentin. "If the Adani Mine Gets Built, It Will Be Thanks to Politicians, on Two Continents. *The Conversation*, May 30, 2019. https://theconversation.com/if-the-adani-mine-gets-built-it-will-be-thanks-to-politicians-on-two-continents-118043.

**Bouman,** Thijs, and Linda Steg. "Motivating Society-Wide Pro-Environmental Change." *One Earth* 1, no. 1 (2019): 27–30.

**Branagan,** Marty. "'We Shall Never Be Moved': Australian Developments in Nonviolence." *Journal of Australian Studies* 27, no. 80 (2003): 201–210.

**Brecher,** Jeremy. *Climate Insurgency: A Strategy for Survival.* Milton Park, Routledge, 2015.

**Burkett,** Maxine. "Climate Disobedience." *Duke Environmental Law & Policy Forum* 27, no. 1 (2016): 1–50.

**Burstein,** Paul, and April Linton. "The Impact of Political Parties, Interest Groups, and Social Movement Organizations on Public Policy: Some Recent Evidence and Theoretical Concerns." *Social Forces* 81, no. 2 (2002): 380–408.

**Callendar,** Guy Stewart. "The Artificial Production of Carbon Dioxide and Its Influence on Temperature." *Quarterly Journal of the Royal Meteorological Society* 64, no. 275 (1938), 223–240.

**Carmin,** JoAnn, and Deborah B. Balser. "Selecting Repertoires of Action in Environmental Movement Organizations: An Interpretive Approach." *Organization and Environment* 15, no. 4 (2002): 365–388.

**Chatterton,** Paul, David Featherstone, and Paul Routledge. "Articulating Climate Justice in Copenhagen: Antagonism, the Commons, and Solidarity." *Antipode* 45, no. 3 (2013): 602–620.

**Chenoweth,** Erica, and Tricia D. Olsen. "Can Civil Resistance Work Against Corporations?" Korbel Quickfacts in Peace and Security. Sié Center for International Security and Diplomacy, Josef Korbel School of International Studies, University of Denver, October 2016. https://www.du.edu/korbel/sie/media/documents/quickfacts-and-policy-briefs/olsen-chenoweth-qf.pdf.

**Chenoweth,** Erica, Evan Perkoski, and Sooyeon Kang. "State Repression and Nonviolent Resistance." *Journal of Conflict Resolution* 61, no. 9 (2017): 1950–1969.

**Climate** Action Tracker. "Australia." September 22, 2020. https://climateactiontracker.org/countries/australia/.

**Coorey,** Phillip. "Charity Faces Loss of Tax Perks for Anti-Coal Campaign." *Financial Review*, December 6, 2017. https://www.afr.com/politics/charity-faces-loss-of-tax-perks-for-anticoal-campaign-20171205-gzyyar.

**Cox,** Robert, and Phaedra C. Pezzullo. *Environmental Communication and the Public Sphere*, 4th ed. Los Angeles: SAGE, 2016.

**Cunningham,** Kathleen Gallagher. "Understanding Strategic Choice: The Determinants of Civil War and Nonviolent Campaign in Self-Determination Disputes." *Journal of Peace Research* 50, no. 3 (2013): 291–304.

**Dalton,** Russell J., Steve Recchia, and Robert Rohrschneider. "The Environmental Movement and the Modes of Political Action." *Comparative Political Studies* 36, no. 7 (2003): 743–772.

**Dawson,** Ashley. "Climate Justice: The Emerging Movement Against Green Capitalism." *South Atlantic Quarterly* 109, no. 2 (2010): 313–338.

**Dean,** Angela J., Robyn Gulliver, and Kerry A. Wilson. "'Taking Action for the Reef?' – Australians Do Not Connect Reef Conservation with Individual Climate Related Actions." *Conservation Letters* 14, no. 2 (March/April 2021): 1–10. https://doi.org/10.1111/conl.12765.

**De Lucia,** Vito. "The Climate Justice Movement and the Hegemonic Discourse of Technology." In *Routledge Handbook of the Climate Change Movement*, edited by Matthias Dietz and Heiko Garrelts, 66–83. Milton Park: Routledge, 2014.

**De Vynck,** Gerrit, Mark Bergen, and Ryan Gallagher. "Google Fires Four Workers, Including Staffer Tied to Protest." *Bloomberg*, November 25, 2019. https://www.bloomberg.com/news/articles/2019-11-25/google-fires-four-employees-citing-data-security-violations.

**Diani,** Mario. "The Concept of Social Movement." *The Sociological Review* 40, no. 1 (1992): 1–25.

**Dudouet,** Véronique. *Powering to Peace: Integrated Civil Resistance and Peacebuilding Strategies*. Washington: ICNC Press, 2017.

**Ekwurzel,** Brenda, James Boneham, Mike W. Dalton, Richard Heede, Roberto J. Mera, Myles R. Allen, and Peter C. Frumhoff. "The Rise in Global Atmospheric CO 2, Surface Temperature, and Sea Level from Emissions Traced to Major Carbon Producers." *Climatic Change* 144, no. 4 (2017): 579–590.

**Feola,** Giuseppe, and Richard Nunes. "Success and Failure of Grassroots Innovations for Addressing Climate Change: The Case of the Transition Movement." *Global Environmental Change* 24 (2014): 232–250.

**Fielding,** Kelly S., and Matthew J. Hornsey. "A Social Identity Analysis of Climate Change and Environmental Attitudes and Behaviors: Insights and Opportunities." *Frontiers in Psychology* 7 (2016): 1–12.

**Fischer,** David, and Richard Baron. "Divestment and Stranded Assets in the Low-Carbon Transition." Background paper for the 32nd Round Table on Sustainable Development, OECD Headquarters, Paris, October 28, 2015. https://www.oecd.org/sd-roundtable/papersandpublications/Divestment%20and%20Stranded%20Assets%20in%20the%20Low-carbon%20Economy%2032nd%20OECD%20RTSD.pdf.

**Fritsche,** Immo, Markus Barth, Philipp Jugert, Torsten Masson, and Gerhard Reese. "A Social Identity Model of Pro-Environmental Action (SIMPEA)." *Psychological Review* 125, no. 2 (2017): 245.

**Gilens,** Martin, and Benjamin I. Page. "Testing Theories of American Politics: Elites, Interest Groups, and Average Citizens." *Perspectives on Politics* 12, no. 3 (2014): 564–581.

**Giugni,** Marco, and Maria T. Grasso. "Environmental Movements in Advanced Industrial Democracies: Heterogeneity, Transformation, and Institutionalization." *Annual Review of Environment and Resources* 40, no. 1 (2015): 337–361. https://doi.org/10.1146/annurev-environ-102014-021327.

**Global** Witness. *At What Cost? Irresponsible Business and the Murder of Land and Environmental Defenders in 2017*. London: Global Witness, 2018.

**Grün,** Bettina, and Kurt Hornik. "topicmodels: An R Package for Fitting Topic Models." *Journal of Statistical Software* 40, no. 13 (May 2011): 1–30. https://doi.org/10.18637/jss.v040.i13.

**Guille,** Howard. "Queensland's Old/New Anti Protest Laws." *Search Foundation*, 2019. https://www.search.org.au/queensland_s_old_new_anti_protest_laws.

**Gulliver,** Robyn, Kelly S. Fielding, and Winnifred R. Louis. "The Characteristics, Activities and Goals of Environmental Organizations Engaged in Advocacy Within the Australian Environmental Movement." *Environmental Communication* 14 no. 5 (2020): 614–627. https://doi.org/10.1080/17524032.2019.1697326.

**Gulliver,** Robyn, Kelly S. Fielding, and Winnifred R. Louis. "Understanding the Outcomes of Climate Change Campaigns in the Australian Environmental Movement." *Case Studies in the Environment* 3, no. 1 (2019): 1–9. https://doi.org/10.1525/cse.2018.001651.

**Hadden,** Jennifer, and Lorien Jasny. "The Power of Peers: How Transnational Advocacy Networks Shape NGO Strategies on Climate Change." *British Journal of Political Science* 49, no. 2 (2019): 637–659.

**Hamilton,** Clive. (2014). "Is Spying on Anti-Coal Activists Just the Tip of the Iceberg?" *The Conversation*, June 4, 2014. https://theconversation.com/is-spying-on-anti-coal-activists-just-the-tip-of-the-iceberg-27570.

**Hill,** Daniel W., and Zachary M. Jones. "An Empirical Evaluation of Explanations for State Repression." *American Political Science Review* 108, no. 3 (2014): 661–687.

**Hornsey,** Matthew J. "Flux in Scepticism Raises Hopes." *Nature Climate Change* 10, no. 4 (2020): 274–275.

**IPCC.** *Global Warming of 1.5°C: An IPCC Special Report on the Impacts of Global Warming of 1.5°C Above Pre-Industrial Levels and Related Global Greenhouse Gas Emission Pathways, in the Context of Strengthening the Global Response to the Threat of Climate Change, Sustainable Development, and Efforts to Eradicate Poverty*. Geneva: World Meteorological Organization, 2018. https://www.ipcc.ch/sr15/.

**Jackson,** Tim. *Prosperity Without Growth: Economics for a Finite Planet*. Milton Park: Routledge, 2009.

**Johnson,** Douglas A., and Nancy L. Pearson. "Tactical Mapping: How Nonprofits Can Identify the Levers of Change." *The Nonprofit Quarterly* 16, no. 2 (2009): 92–99.

**Jugert,** Philipp, Katharine H. Greenaway, Markus Barth, Ronja Büchner, Sarah Eisentraut, and Immo Fritsche. "Collective Efficacy Increases Pro-Environmental Intentions Through Increasing Self-Efficacy." *Journal of Environmental Psychology* 48 (2016): 12–23.

**Karena,** Cynthia. "Environmental Education in Australian Schools." *ECOS* 155 (2010). http://www.ecosmagazine.com/print/EC155p16.htm.

**Kirkwood,** Ian. "Climate Group 350.org Investigated over 2016 Newcastle Harbour Coal Protest." *Bendigo Advertiser*, December 11, 2017. https://www.bendigoadvertiser.com.au/story/5114281/climate-group-investigated-over-2016-protest/.

**Klandermans,** Pieter Gijsbertus. *The Social Psychology of Protest*. Oxford: Blackwell, 1997.

**Knaus,** Christopher. "Fossil-Fuel Industry Doubles Donations to Major Parties in Four Years, Report Shows." *The Guardian*, February 12, 2020. https://www.theguardian.com/environment/2020/feb/12/fossil-fuel-industry-doubles-donations-to-major-parties-in-four-years-report-shows.

**Korbel,** Andrew. "A New Era of Climate Change Litigation in Australia?" *Corrs Chambers Westgarth*, April 8, 2019. https://corrs.com.au/insights/a-new-era-of-climate-change-litigation-in-australia.

**Kössler,** Georg. "The Climate Movement in Germany." In *Routledge Handbook of the Climate Change Movement*, edited by Matthias Dietz and Heiko Garrelts, 117–130. Milton Park: Routledge, 2014.

**Lampert,** Martijn, S. Sander Metaal, Sheng Liu, and Laura Gambarin. *Global Rise in Environmental Concern: World Population Waking Up to the Ecological Crisis.* Amsterdam: Glocalities, 2019. https://www.courthousenews.com/wp-content/uploads/2019/08/ClimateChangeGlocalities.pdf.

**Lander,** Edgardo, Walden Bello, Ulrich Brand, Nicola Bullard, and Tadzio Mueller. *Contours of Climate Justice: Ideas for Shaping New Climate and Energy Politics.* Uppsala: Dag Hammarskjöld Foundation, 2009.

**Lange,** Glenn-Marie, Quentin Wodon, and Kevin Carey, eds. *The Changing Wealth of Nations 2018: Building a Sustainable Future.* Washington: World Bank Publications, 2018.

**Laureates** Open Letter, 2020. "An Open Letter on Australian Bushfires and Climate: Urgent Need for Deep Cuts in Carbon Emissions." https://laureatebushfiresclimate.wordpress.com/.

**Lee,** Julian. "Barbie Gets Dumped for Being an Environmental Wrecker." *Sydney Morning Herald*, June 8, 2011. https://www.smh.com.au/environment/conservation/barbie-gets-dumped-for-being-an-environmental-wrecker-20110607-1fr4i.html.

**Leggett,** Jeremy. *Climate Change and the Insurance Industry: Solidarity Among the Risk Community?* Greenpeace, 1993.

**Long,** Stephen. "Adani Carmichael Coal Mine: Former Indian Minister Sounds Alarm on Adani's Track Record, Mega-Mine's Viability." *ABC News*, October 1, 2017. http://www.abc.net.au/news/2017-10-02/former-minister-sounds-alarm-on-adanistrack-record-in-india/9005596.

**Louis,** Winnifred R. "Collective Action—And Then What?" *Journal of Social Issues* 65, no. 4 (2009): 727–748.

**Louis,** Winnifred R., and Cristina Jayme Montiel. "Social Movements and Social Transformation: Steps Towards Understanding the Challenges and Breakthroughs of Social Change." *Peace and Conflict: Journal of Peace Psychology* 24, no. 1 (2018): 3.

**Louis,** Winnifred, Emma Thomas, Craig McGarty, Morgana Lizzio-Wilson, Catherine Amiot, and Fathali Moghaddam. "The Volatility of Collective Action: Theoretical Analysis and Empirical Data." *Political Psychology* 41 (2020): 35–74.

**Macy,** Joanna. *World as Self, World as Lover: Courage for Global Justice and Ecological Renewal.* Berkeley: Parallax Press, 2007.

**Manheim,** Jarol B. "The Death of a Thousand Cuts." *Institute of Public Affairs* 53, no. 1 (2001): 3–6.

**Martin,** Brian. "From Political Jiu-Jitsu to the Backfire Dynamic: How Repression Can Promote Mobilization." In *Civil Resistance: Comparative Perspectives on Nonviolent Struggle*, edited by Kurt Schock, 145–167. Minneapolis: University of Minneapolis Press, 2015.

**Massola,** James. "Big Surge in Opposition to Adani, New Polling Reveals." *Sydney Morning Herald*, February 1, 2018. **https://www.smh.com.au/politics/federal/big-surge-in-opposition-to-adani-new-polling-reveals-20180131-p4yz4o.html**.

**McAdam,** Doug. *Political Process and the Development of Black Insurgency, 1930–1970*. Chicago: University of Chicago Press, 1982.

**McAdam,** Doug. "Social Movement Theory and the Prospects for Climate Change Activism in the United States." *Annual Review of Political Science* 20 (2017): 189–208.

**McAdam,** Doug, John D. McCarthy, and Mayer N. Zald. *Comparative Perspectives on Social Movements: Political Opportunities, Mobilizing Structures, and Cultural Framings*. Cambridge: Cambridge University Press, 1996.

**McCarthy,** John D., and Mayer N. Zald. "Resource Mobilization and Social Movements: A Partial Theory." *American Journal of Sociology* 82, no. 6 (1977): 1212–1241.

**McCright,** Aaron M., and Riley E. Dunlap. "The Nature and Social Bases of Progressive Social Movement Ideology: Examining Public Opinion Toward Social Movements." *The Sociological Quarterly* 49, no. 4 (2008): 825–848.

**McKibben,** Bill. "Global Warming's Terrifying New Math. *Rolling Stone* 19, no. 7 (2012).

**Meredith,** Sam. "British Police Issue a City-Wide Ban on Climate Change Protests in London." *CNBC*, October 15, 2019. **https://www.cnbc.com/2019/10/15/extinction-rebellion-climate-change-protests-banned-in-london-by-police.html**.

**Merriam-Webster.** Accessed August 2, 2021. **https://www.merriam-webster.com/**.

**Meyer,** David. S. "Protest and Political Opportunities." *Annual Review Sociology* 30 (2004): 125–145.

**Mogus,** Jason, and Tom Liacas. *Networked Change: How Progressive Campaigns Are Won in the 21st Century*. Salt Spring Island: NetChange, 2016.

**Molley,** Shannon. "Extinction Rebellion Climate Change Protests Doing 'More Harm Than Good.'" *News.com.au*, October 9, 2019. **https://www.news.com.au/technology/environment/climate-change/extinction-rebellion-climate-change-protests-doing-more-harm-than-good/news-story/a07617ee3ba5b2f8ace3c-9c910802df2**.

**Moser,** Susanne C. "In the Long Shadows of Inaction: The Quiet Building of a Climate Protection Movement in the United States." *Global Environmental Politics* 7, no. 2 (2007): 124–144. **https://doi.org/10.1162/glep.2007.7.2.124**.

**Moskalenko,** Sophia, and Clark McCauley. "Measuring Political Mobilization: The Distinction Between Activism and Radicalism." *Terrorism and Political Violence* 21, no. 2 (2009): 239–260.

**Nisbet,** Matthew C. "Communicating Climate Change: Why Frames Matter for Public Engagement." *Environment: Science and Policy for Sustainable Development* 51, no. 2 (2009): 12–23. **https://doi.org/10.3200/ENVT.51.2.12-23**.

**O'Brien,** Thomas. "Fragmentation or Evolution? Understanding Change Within the New Zealand Environmental Movement." *Journal of Civil Society* 9, no. 3 (2013): 287–299. **https://doi.org/10.1080/17448689.2013.818267**.

**Oreskes,** Naomi, and Erik M. Conway. *Merchants of Doubt: How a Handful of Scientists Obscured the Truth on Issues from Tobacco Smoke to Global Warming.* New York: Bloomsbury Publishing USA, 2011.

**Our Community.** "Help Sheet: Legal Structuring." *Ourcommunity.com.au*, n.d. Accessed August 2, 2021. https://www.ourcommunity.com.au/management/view_help_sheet.do?articleid=733.

**Oxford** Reference. "Overview: Counter-Mobilization," 2021. https://www.oxfordreference.com/view/10.1093/oi/authority.20110803095643890.

**Paris,** Nicola. "Suppression Of the Right to Protest." *Green Agenda*, April 29, 2019. https://greenagenda.org.au/2019/04/right-to-protest/.

**Pearse,** Rebecca. "Moving Targets: Carbon Pricing, Energy Markets, and Social Movements in Australia." *Environmental Politics* 25, no. 6 (2016): 1079–1101. https://doi.org/10.1080/09644016.2016.1196969.

**Pennebaker,** James W., Ryan L. Boyd, Kayla Jordan, and Kate Blackburn. *The Development and Psychometric Properties of LIWC2015.* Austin: University of Texas at Austin, 2015. https://repositories.lib.utexas.edu/bitstream/handle/2152/31333/LIWC2015_LanguageManual.pdf.

**Polletta,** Francesca. "Culture and Movements." *The ANNALS of the American Academy of Political and Social Science* 619, no. 1 (2008): 78–96.

**Popovic,** Srdja, Slobodan Djinovic, Andrej Milivojevic, Hardy Merriman, and Ivan Marovic. *CANVAS Core Curriculum: A Guide to Effective Nonviolent Struggle.* Belgrade: CANVAS, 2007.

**Porta,** Donatella, and Dieter Rucht. "The Dynamics of Environmental Campaigns." *Mobilization: An International Quarterly* 7, no. 1 (2002): 1–14.

**Poulos,** Helen M., and Mary Alice Haddad. "Violent Repression of Environmental Protests." *SpringerPlus* 5, no. 1 (2016): 230.

**Power,** Clare. "Transition: A Force in the Great Turning?" PhD diss., University of Western Sydney (Australia), 2015.

**R Core Team.** *R: A Language and Environment for Statistical Computing.* Vienna, Austria: R Foundation for Statistical Computing, 2013.

**Rennie,** George. "Lobbying 101: How Interest Groups Influence Politicians and the Public to Get What They Want." *The Conversation*, June 8, 2016. https://theconversation.com/lobbying-101-how-interest-groups-influence-politicians-and-the-public-to-get-what-they-want-60569.

**Rich,** Nathaniel. "Losing Earth: The Decade We Almost Stopped Climate Change." *New York Times Magazine*, August 1, 2018.

**Richards,** John P., and Jack Heard. "European Environmental NGOs: Issues, Resources and Strategies in Marine Campaigns." *Environmental Politics* 14 no. 1 (2005): 23–41. https://doi.org/10.1080/09644401042000310169.

**Ripple,** William J., Christopher Wolf, Thomas M. Newsome, Mauro Galetti, Mohammed Alamgir, Eileen Crist, Mahmoud I. Mahmoud, William F. Laurance, and 15,364 Scientist Signatories from 184 Countries. "World Scientists' Warning to Humanity: A Second Notice." *BioScience* 67, no. 12 (2017): 1026–1028.

**Ritter,** Daniel P. "Civil Resistance." In *The Oxford Handbook of Social Movements*, edited by Donatella Della Porta and Mario Diani, 467–478. Oxford: Oxford University Press, 2015.

**Ritter,** David. *The Coal Truth: The Fight to Stop Adani, Defeat the Big Polluters and Reclaim Our Democracy*. Perth: University of Western Australia Press, 2018.

**Russo,** Katherine. E. "Stop Adani: Risk Communication and Legal Mining Conflicts in Australian Media Discourse." *Anglistica AION: An Interdisciplinary Journal* 22, no. 1 (2018): 7–23.

**Saunders,** Amanda. "Coal-Mining Lobby Says Anti-Investment Campaign May Be Illegal." *Financial Review*, June 23, 2014. https://www.afr.com/companies/mining/coal-mining-lobby-says-anti-investment-campaign-may-be-illegal-20140623-je1s1.

**Schäfer,** Mike S. "Online Communication on Climate Change and Climate Politics: A Literature Review." *Wiley Interdisciplinary Reviews: Climate Change* 3, no. 6 (2012): 527–543.

**Schlosberg,** David, and Lisette B. Collins. "From Environmental to Climate Justice: Climate Change and the Discourse of Environmental Justice." *Wiley Interdisciplinary Reviews: Climate Change* 5, no. 3 (2014): 359–374.

**Schomberg,** William and Simon Dawson. "UK Police Arrest 10 Climate Activists Before Protests." *Reuters*, October 5, 2019. https://www.reuters.com/article/us-climate-change-britain/uk-police-arrest-10-climate-activists-before-protests-idUSKCN1WK0C7.

**Seccombe,** Mike. "Activism and Secondary Boycotts." *The Saturday Paper*, November 9, 2019. https://www.thesaturdaypaper.com.au/news/politics/2019/11/09/activism-and-secondary-boycotts/15732180009057.

**Sengupta,** Somini, and Nadja Popovich. "More Than 60 Countries Say They'll Zero Out Carbon Emissions. The Catch? They're Not the Big Emitters." *The New York Times*, September 25, 2019. https://www.nytimes.com/interactive/2019/09/25/climate/un-net-zero-emissions.html.

**Seyfang,** Gill. *The New Economics of Sustainable Consumption: Seeds of Change*. New York: Palgrave Macmillan, 2009.

**Sharp,** Gene. *The Politics of Nonviolent Action, Vol. 1*. Boston: Porter Sargent Publisher, 1973.

**Smith,** Jackie, and Jacqueline Patterson. "Global Climate Justice Activism: 'The New Protagonists' and Their Projects for a Just Transition." In *Ecologically Unequal Exchange: Environmental Justice in Comparative and Historical Perspective*, edited by R. Scott Frey, Paul K. Gellert, and Harry Dahms, 245–272. New York: Palgrave Macmillan, 2019.

**Stanton,** Kate. "Waging a Legal Battle on Climate Change." *MLS News* 21 (June 2019). https://law.unimelb.edu.au/alumni/mls-news/issue-21-june-2019/waging-a-legal-battle-on-climate-change.

**Tarrow,** Sidney G. *Power in Movement: Social Movements and Contentious Politics*. Cambridge: Cambridge University Press, 2011.

**Tausch,** Nicole, Julia C. Becker, Russell Spears, Oliver Christ, Rim Saab, Purnima Singh, and Roomana N. Siddiqui. "Explaining Radical Group Behavior: Developing Emotion and Efficacy Routes to Normative and Nonnormative Collective Action." *Journal of Personality and Social Psychology* 101, no. 1 (2011): 129–148. https://doi.org/10.1037/a0022728.

**Taylor,** Lenore. "Coal from Carmichael Mine 'Will Create More Annual Emissions than New York.'" *The Guardian*, November 12, 2015. https://www.theguardian.com/environment/2015/nov/12/coal-from-carmichael-mine-will-create-more-annual-emissions-than-new-york.

**The Australia Institute.** *Polling – Changing Climate Change Concern and Attitudes*. January 2020. https://www.tai.org.au/sites/default/files/Polling%20-%20January%202020%20-%20Climate%20change%20concern%20and%20attitude%20%5BWeb%5D.pdf.

**Lowy** Institute. "Australian Attitudes to Climate Change." Lowyinstitute.org, no date. **https://interactives.lowyinstitute.org/features/australian-attitudes-to-climate-change/**.

**Tilly,** Charles. *From Mobilization to Revolution.* New York: Random House, 1978.

**Trenorden,** Christine. "Environmental Legal Aid Slashed When Australia Needs It Most." *The Conversation*, March 11, 2014.

**Uluğ,** Özden Melis, and Yasemin Gülsüm Acar. "What Happens After the Protests? Understanding Protest Outcomes Through Multi-Level Social Change." *Peace and Conflict: Journal of Peace Psychology* 24, no. 1 (2018): 44.

**UN Women.** "Setting the Campaign Objectives or Desired Outcomes." January 3, 2012. **https://www.endvawnow.org/en/articles/1201-setting-the-campaign-objectives-or-desired-outcomes.html**.

**United** Nations. "Ten Impacts of the Australian Bushfires." UN Environment Programme, January 22, 2020. **https://www.unenvironment.org/news-and-stories/story/ten-impacts-australian-bushfires**.

**Van Dijk,** Albert I. J. M., Hylke E. Beck, Russell S. Crosbie, Richard A. M. de Jeu, Yi Y. Liu, Geoff M. Podger, Bertrand Timbal, and Neil R. Viney. "The Millennium Drought in Southeast Australia (2001–2009): Natural and Human Causes and Implications for Water Resources, Ecosystems, Economy, and Society." *Water Resources Research* 49, no. 2 (2013): 1040–1057.

**Vining,** Peter. "Democratic Repression of Non-Violent Activist Groups and the Likelihood of Political Violence." Paper 29, Southern Illinois University Carbondale OPENSIUC, Summer 2011.

**Walker,** Edward T., Andrew W. Martin, and John D. McCarthy. "Confronting the State, the Corporation, and the Academy: The Influence of Institutional Targets on Social Movement Repertoires." *American Journal of Sociology* 114, no. 1 (2008): 35–76.

**Wallan,** Scout. "Climate Activists Refused Bail." *EchoNet Daily*, December 6, 2019. **https://www.echo.net.au/2019/12/climate-activists-refused-bail/**.

**White,** Anna. "The Movement of Movements: From Resistance to Climate Justice." *Common Dreams*, December 10, 2009. **https://sharing.org/information-centre/blogs/movement-movements-resistance-climate-justice**.

**Wicker,** Alden. "Conscious Consumerism Is a Lie. Here's a Better Way to Help Save the World." *Quartz*, March 1, 2017. **https://qz.com/920561/conscious-consumerism-is-a-lie-heres-a-better-way-to-help-save-the-world/**.

**Wilson Becerril,** Michael S. "Mining Conflicts in Peru: Civil Resistance and Corporate Counterinsurgency." *Journal of Resistance Studies* 4, no. 1 (2018): 94–127.

**Wordsworth,** Matt. "Will Queensland's Dangerous Devices Laws Stop Extinction Rebellion Protests?" *ABC News*, October 19, 2019. **https://www.abc.net.au/news/2019-10-19/queensland-dangerous-devices-laws-targeting-protest-movement/11617422/**

**Wright,** Stephen C., Donald M. Taylor, and Fathali M. Moghaddam. "Responding to Membership in a Disadvantaged Group: From Acceptance to Collective Protest." *Journal of Personality and Social Psychology* 58, no. 6 (1990): 994–1003.

**XR Aus.** "21 Yr Old Activist Hit with Highest Environmental Fine in Australian History." *Extinction Rebellion*, April 4, 2019. **https://ausrebellion.earth/news/21-yr-old-activist-hit-with-highest-environmental-fine-in-australian-history/**.

**Zchout,** Shira Leon, and Alon Tal. "Conflict Versus Consensus Strategic Orientations Among Environmental NGOs: An Empirical Evaluation." *Voluntas* 28, no. 3 (2017): 1110–1134.

# Methodological Appendix

This appendix describes in detail the approaches used to collect and analyze data for each of the chapters in the monograph. We describe the methodology used to construct each of the five databases listed in Table 2: "Groups," "Campaigns," "Tactics," "Civil resistance," and "Outcomes."

### Groups Database: Identification of Australian Groups Focusing on Environmental Advocacy

The first stage of developing the database of Australian groups involved in climate change civil resistance involved identifying the population of groups active across all issues within the Australian environmental movement in 2017. To do this we identified potential groups by reviewing the Australian Register of Environmental Organisations (Australian Government 2018) and then using a snowball search system to follow linked groups and networks where listed. This process resulted in the development of a pool of 2,668 potential groups, which were then manually checked for the presence of an active website with a focus on national environmental issues. Applying these inclusion criteria resulted in 1,373 websites selected for more detailed review. These were then further filtered to only include those groups who undertook some form of environmental activism. We operationalized the word "activism" by applying the definition used by the Australian Federal Government through the Australian Charities and Not-for-profits Commission (ACNC). This entity governs charitable organizations engaging in social and environmental change in Australia. The ACNC groups these activities as "advocacy," defined as "activities which are aimed at securing or opposing any change to a law, policy or practice in the Commonwealth, a state or territory, or another country" (Australian Government 2012, 1). These activities are grouped by the ACNC into campaigning, lobbying, and general advocacy. Thus, the three words "campaign," "advocate" (including variants), and "lobby" were chosen as the search terms for identifying organizations in the dataset engaged in environmental activism.

A manual search of each individual site using the three keywords was undertaken via the online site-provided search tool. Groups that did not return any positive search results, or did not provide an internal site search option, were then manually searched on the "About," "What we do," or equivalent webpage for a selected range of other terms related to advocacy and civil resistance. These included terms such as "influence," "fight," "movement," or "take action," as well as phrases which express any activities related to changing laws, policies, or practices. As a result of this process a further 876 groups were removed as they were judged not to undertake any form of environmental advocacy nor civil resistance (following Andrews, et al. 2016). The largest sub-group removed from the population were those working in "environmental remediation," for example, through wildlife rescue or the restoration of bushland.

The final sample for analysis was 492 websites that were downloaded between December 5, 2016, and April 30, 2017, into static form for coding via Adobe Acrobat's multi-level website-to-PDF conversion tool. Downloaded content included all webpages for each organization, online actions such as petitions, declarations, and emails, and news and blog posts back dated from January 1, 2016, to the date of individual download. Downloadable reports that had been authored by the target organization were included alongside annual, financial, and presidents' (or their equivalent) reports. Audiovisual material was not downloaded, nor were social media sites or other external platform content. Each of the 492 Adobe files were then cleaned. External website pages were manually removed, as were any petitions, reports, or submissions authored by external parties. Repetitious footers and page duplications were removed to avoid unduly influencing text and linguistic analysis output values. The process created 62,516 pages of website content for analysis, with websites ranging from 5 to 1,500 pages in length.

Codable attributes for content analysis were identified from the research literature on environmental activism and communication about issue focus, events, campaign goals, and campaign targets. This was done in order to construct a database specifically for groups focused on climate change activism and to develop the campaigns database. To identify data for each of these attributes we created keywords (e.g., "campaign"). We then searched through the scraped website text to find incidents where these words were used. Inter-coder reliability was established through a staged approach, testing two coders' results after 10, 30, and 50 documents were coded. Discrepancies of <0.60 in inter-coder reliability were reconciled at each stage through discussion, with 100% agreement reached between the two coders. A total of 50 websites were dual coded, resulting in a 10% sample percentage which is suitable for online content coding (Joyce 2018; Lombard, Snyder-Duch, and Bracken 2002). The remaining 90% of the data was then coded by one person. The final average inter-coder reliability was 0.809 (Krippendorff's Alpha) and 0.81 (Cohen's Kappa), which are considered acceptable (Hayes and Krippendorff 2007).

In order to use updated website text for the monograph sections on framing (see Chapter 2) we re-scraped the websites in our Groups study population in early 2020. We did not undertake any manual coding on this text; however, we did use the text corpus for text analysis using the Linguistic Inquiry and Word Count program (Pennebaker, et al. 2015) and R software for topic modeling (Grün and Hornik 2011).

## Campaigns and Outcomes Databases: Identification of Climate Change-Related Campaigns and Their Outcomes

As described above, the website content from each group in the Group Database was read to identify campaign names, issue, goals, and targets. Campaigns which were organized by groups focusing on climate change were included in this database, as well as climate-focused campaigns run by other environmental groups. In total, 193 campaigns were identified.

An online search was undertaken in early 2020 to identify whether the goals of the campaigns have been achieved. This search was done with Google search engine using different combinations of the campaign name, goal, or group responsible for its implementation. This assessment process involved searching for news stories, reports, or any data available online indicating whether the goal of the campaign had been achieved. Each campaign was then assessed as achieving either a "successful," "partially successful," "unsuccessful," or "unknown" outcome. It is important to note that this process does not enable claims of causation between the activities of each group and the particular outcomes which were identified.

Successful campaigns are those that achieved their goal. For example, a campaign targeting a university to divest from fossil fuels was assessed as successful if the university made a formal, public commitment to do so. Likewise, a campaign was deemed unsuccessful if the goal had not been achieved. For example, a campaign to stop a coal mine would be considered unsuccessful if the coal mine proceeded or continued to progress in its approval or construction process. Partially successful campaigns were those with possibly multiple goals or targets, of which one or more were achieved. The outcomes of campaigns targeting changes in behavior, such as reducing the amount of meat an individual eats, were unable to be assessed because data on individual behavior (e.g., meat consumption) in the areas targeted by those campaigns is unavailable.

## Tactics Database: Categorization of All Tactics Used by Environmental Groups in the Study Population

In order to find out what climate change civil resistance tactics are used across these groups in the database, we collected data on the events promoted by each of the groups on their Facebook pages and groups. We undertook this process in two different ways. Our first approach was to identify events by reviewing each group's website to check for event listings. This method resulted in the identification of a total of 799 events from 2017. Two limitations of this approach were observed: First, many groups did not appear to update their new events on their websites. In fact, 188 (37.83%) of the 492 groups did not appear to have updated any part of their website in the previous 200 days. Second, where website events were updated, information about past events was often removed. This impacted the representativeness of the event data acquired. As a result, we chose to exclusively use Facebook event data in the second round of data gathering. In this round, event data was scraped from each group's Facebook page, capturing all listed events up until December 31, 2019. As we are interested in events which involve the mobilization of supporters, Facebook offers a cost-effective and accessible forum for promoting these events publicly. In addition, Facebook records all past events, thus enabling the acquisition of a detailed and representative dataset and removing the need to use events identified from websites.

In order to acquire this information, each group in the study population was searched for on Facebook to identify whether they had a public Facebook page or group. While pages and groups operate slightly differently, they can both be used to promote group events. Where a group had events listed, these events were manually copied, with the data compiled into a large Tactics database. Some organizations had multiple Facebook pages, for example Extinction Rebellion, which had 74 separate Facebook accounts by January 1, 2020. In total, 728 Facebook pages and groups were found. Scraping each of them generated a total of 36,541 events running from June 2010 to January 2020. Of these events, 8,607 were cohosted. This occurs when two or more groups list the event on their Facebook page. Throughout this monograph we have used either the full dataset of all events (36,541) where suitable, or specified when only the unique events (i.e., the event database with cohosted duplicates removed) were included in the analysis. This approach was used since it is very difficult to identify which of the cohosts was the primary organizer of the event.

Following this process, three subsets were then created for use in this monograph. The first subset identified all events promoted by groups active on climate change issues. Events promoted by groups which focused on other issues were reviewed, and any individual events focusing on climate change were added to the climate change tactics dataset. Similarly, two subsets were created for the Divestment and Stop Adani campaigns. The Divestment and Stop Adani subsets were created in two steps. First, we compiled all events undertaken by groups primarily focused on each campaign: events organized by all Stop Adani sub-groups, Frontline Action on Coal, and Galilee Blockade for the Stop Adani campaign, and Fossil Free and 350.org sub-groups for the Divestment campaign. We then added events from the overall events database which also had the word "Adani" or "divest" in the event title. This resulted in a dataset of 3,339 events in the Stop Adani event dataset (of which 2,221 were unique) and 1,571 events in the Divestment event dataset (of which 1,407 were unique).

## Civil Resistance Tactics Database: Identification and Categorization of Civil Resistance Tactics

As highlighted when discussing the Tactics database, events were originally captured from the websites which were scraped in 2017. We then coded these events by event name (i.e., "film screening") and inductively grouped into five event types: civil resistance tactics, meetings/administration, information sharing, eco-activities, and social/fundraising. The civil resistance tactics category includes all events that involve some form of physical protest, rally, demonstration, or similar, as per Beer's typology. In our second round of data capture using Facebook pages, we used the same process. Given that the dataset was very large (36,541 events) we first used an excel macro to identify keywords in each event title (e.g., "film," "movie," or "screening" were all grouped as "film screenings"). Events which did not return an easily categorized event type were then manually reviewed and grouped. Finally, all 6,393 civil resistance tactics were manually reviewed and categorized. These were then matched against Beer's (2021) categories of civil resistance tactics (see Table 1).

## About the Authors

**Robyn Gulliver** is a multi-award winning environmentalist, writer, and researcher who has served as an organizer and leader of numerous local and national environmental organizations. Born in New Zealand, she has spent the last decade advocating for and writing about environmental issues for activist groups, local councils, not-for-profit organizations, and academia.

**Kelly S. Fielding** is a Professor of Environmental Psychology at the University of Queensland in the School of Communication and Arts. Her research focuses broadly on understanding the social and psychological determinants of environmental sustainability. She seeks to understand environmental decisions and behaviors and to develop communication and behavior change strategies that can promote greater environmental sustainability.

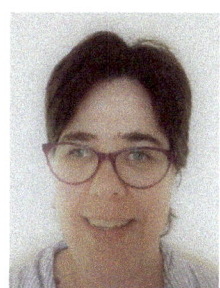

**Winnifred R. Louis** is a Professor of Psychology at the University of Queensland, Australia. Her research interests focus on the influence of identity and norms on social decision-making. She has studied this broad topic in contexts from political activism to peace psychology to health and the environment.